HOW DO YOU LEARN?
HOW DO YOU THINK?
WHAT ARE YOUR HOBBIES?
WHAT WILL YOU EARN?
WHO WILL YOU LOVE?

Your blood type is a powerful indicator of the under-lying traits which affect every aspect of your life. Now this breakthrough book gives you access to your inher-ited behavior patterns, strengths and weaknesses, talents and dangerous tendencies in all the areas of daily living. If you have ever wondered . . .

- Why do I feel anxious around strangers?
- What makes him save and me always spend?
- Why does she get things done and I don't?
- What's the secret behind making money?
- Why can't I get my lover to talk about feelings?

THE SELF-KNOWLEDGE YOU SEEK
LIES IN YOUR LIFE'S BLOOD.

WHAT'S
YOUR
TYPE?

PETER CONSTANTINE is the author of numerous books on Japanese and Far Eastern language and culture. He has also done a number of pieces in such magazines as *The New Yorker, Details, Arena,* and *Harvard Magazine,* as well as scholarly magazines. He is continuing his research on biopsychology for a book on blood types and relationships. He lives in New York City.

WHAT'S YOUR TYPE?

HOW BLOOD TYPES
ARE THE KEYS TO
UNLOCKING YOUR
PERSONALITY

Peter Constantine

A PLUME BOOK

PLUME
Published by the Penguin Group
Penguin Books USA Inc., 375 Hudson Street,
New York, New York 10014, U.S.A.
Penguin Books Ltd, 27 Wrights Lane, London W8 5TZ, England
Penguin Books Australia Ltd, Ringwood, Victoria, Australia
Penguin Books Canada Ltd, 10 Alcorn Avenue, Toronto, Ontario, Canada M4V 3B2
Penguin Books (N.Z.) Ltd, 182–190 Wairau Road, Auckland 10, New Zealand

Penguin Books Ltd, Registered Offices:
Harmondsworth, Middlesex, England

First published by Plume, an imprint of Dutton Signet,
a division of Penguin Books USA Inc.

First Printing, July, 1997
10 9 8 7 6 5 4 3 2 1

 REGISTERED TRADEMARK—MARCA REGISTRADA

LIBRARY OF CONGRESS CATALOGING-IN-PUBLICATION DATA:
Constantine, Peter.
What's your type? : how blood types are the keys to unlocking your personality / Peter
Constantine.
p.   cm.
ISBN 0-452-27802-3
1. Typology (Psychology) 2. Blood groups—Psychological aspects.
I. Title.
BF698.3.C66   1997
155.2'34—dc21
                                                                                    97-587
                                                                                       CIP

Printed in the United States of America
Set in New Baskerville
Designed by Jesse Cohen

BOOKS ARE AVAILABLE AT QUANTITY DISCOUNTS WHEN USED TO PROMOTE PRODUCTS OR SERVICES.
FOR INFORMATION PLEASE WRITE TO PREMIUM MARKETING DIVISION, PENGUIN BOOKS USA INC.,
375 HUDSON STREET, NEW YORK, NEW YORK 10014.

ACKNOWLEDGMENTS

I would like to thank the many people who have helped make this book possible, especially the individuals from the different blood groups, some of whom have wished to remain anonymous. Their open, interesting, and revealing discussions have been of enormous benefit. Their information has enabled me to put a human perspective on much of the scientific material.

I owe the greatest thanks to Burton Pike for his help, inspiration, and advice, and to my agent Jessica Wainwright for encouraging me to write this book. I am also very grateful to my editor, Danielle Perez, for her help and support.

I would also like to thank Mark Peterson for his advice and his input on "O" characteristics.

INTRODUCTION

Did you know that your blood type—A, B, O, or AB—determines how you think, feel, work, and play?

Scientists throughout the world have produced extensive evidence of the genetic link between personality and blood groups. Each group has deep-lying traits that affect every aspect of your life. Whether you are A, B, O, or AB, you have your own way of learning, loving, relating to people, even dealing with money.

At some time or other we have all stopped and wondered:

Why do I feel so anxious when I'm around people
   I don't know?
Why are the two of us not communicating?
Why does she get things done and I don't?
What's the secret behind his golden touch?
Why do I panic about money?

The answers to these questions and many more lie in our blood.

For more than sixty-five years, scientists and biopsychologists have studied thousands upon thousands of people, and the results of their research paint crystal-clear pictures of the traits we carry in our blood and hand down from one generation to the next. If both your parents are A's, then so are you—and deep down you're just like them. If your mother is an AB and your father an O, then you might be an A or a B—very different from them in temperament. "Blood," the Japanese expert Toshitaka Nomi says, "is much more than the vital fluid that carries oxygen and other necessary life-supporting nutrients through your cardiovascular system."

What's Your Type? lays out the science of how you and the people around you think and feel, and why you do the things you do. Each chapter looks at a different area of life and probes deeply into the behavior patterns, the strengths and weaknesses, of each blood type. Throughout the book we meet people from different blood groups who speak openly about their hopes and worries, about how they work, play, and love, about how they meet people, and about how they deal with relationships. Quotes from biopsychologists in France, Switzerland, Germany, Japan, and China present the scientific evidence.

As you move from chapter to chapter, your insight into what makes a certain blood type tick will become sharper, and spotting who's who in the crowd will become easier. In the eighties, during my research for my books on Japan, I was continually taken aback when Japanese people were able to pinpoint my blood type—sometimes even within a few minutes after meeting me.

The principle behind *What's Your Type?* is that knowledge is power. Understanding why you feel the way you do in a situation, or why a friend suddenly rejects you and a stranger suddenly takes to you, makes life easier.

But how did all this start?

In 1901, Dr. Karl Landsteiner, who later won the Nobel Prize, identified the four blood groups to which we all belong, revolutionizing the world's view of man's biochemical makeup. Reliable blood transfusions were now possible without the dangers of the violent and often fatal reactions that occur when blood from incompatible groups combines. Then, in 1910, von Dungern and Hirszfeld began researching the genetics of blood. They identified the inherited patterns, isolating independent pairs of genes that transmit blood type from parents to children.

The first links between personality and blood groups were made by the Japanese psychologist Takeji Furukawa, who published his findings in the German *Journal of Applied Psychology* in 1931. The German psychologist Karl H. Göbber took Furukawa's work further, widening the research in scope and depth. In Switzerland, Dr. K. Fritz Schaer had begun independently researching personality and blood groups, using the students of the Swiss Military Academy as test subjects.

In France, Jacques Genevay and Léone Bourdel were publishing their own groundbreaking scientific work, and throughout the fifties, sixties, and seventies Brazilian, Russian, Japanese, Chinese, Australian, and American specialists extended blood group psychology into the fields of education, psychiatry, medicine, and even criminology.

Blood group psychology has come a long way since the pioneering days of the thirties. Interestingly enough, it has developed in two separate directions: east and west.

In the West, in Europe, South America, and the United States, blood group biopsychology has remained within the strict confines of the medical laboratory. Western readers interested in the subject have had to plow through technical journals of hematology, psychiatry, immunogenetics, and serology.

But in the East, in Japan and China, blood type psychology has reached the masses. Tell the first Japanese person you meet "I'm an AB, what do you think about that?" and you will probably be surprised at his or her unrelentingly clear character portrayal of you. How can this perfect stranger, you might wonder, see right through me, know my strengths and my hang-ups?

The answer is that since the seventies hundreds of popular

books have kept the Japanese public abreast of the latest developments in blood group psychology. What in the West has stayed locked up in the highly specialized world of hematological and psychiatric science has in Japan been laid out in plain language. In the past two decades, the father and son team of Masahiko Nomi and Toshitaka Nomi have done extensive work on blood type psychology, following men and women of all ages in their activities every minute of the day. Their verdict: Your blood type affects *everything* you do, from how you cook to how you love to how you play golf.

But in many ways Western specialists have outdone the Japanese in the directions they have taken in their research. While Japan's Nomi clan works on a popular level, investigating fun bits like "why most Tokyo chefs happen to be B's," Western experts have moved into more delicate terrain. On the American scene we find articles with the following titles:

> "Effects of Stress and Blood Type on Cortisol and VLD Toxicity"
> "Affective Disorders and ABO Blood Groups: New Data and a Re-analysis of the Literature Using the Logistic Transformation of Proportions"
> "The Influence of Stress and Blood Type on Toxicity-preventing Activity and Other Cardiac Risk Factors"

Today, Western scientists are studying the relation of blood groups to everything from smoking and drinking to susceptibility to cancer. The *Irish Journal of Psychological Medicine* even published data on blood groups and dementia.

What has made blood group psychology Japan's leading popular science is that it *is* a science: There is clear-cut statistical, even clinical, proof that backs up the popular theories. The Japanese argue that astrology, enneagrams, even Jungian typology are all too often simply based on conjecture. What proof is there, a Japanese acquaintance asked me, whether Virgo or Taurus are compatible or not, or that they tend to react this way or that way? "With blood types," she pointed out, "the core of, say, the AB personality, or the O personality, is completely immutable. If you are an O, then deep down you *are* an O—there's no escaping it!"

The ratio of blood groups differs from one country to another. In the United States and Great Britain, for instance, four people in ten are O's, and about three in ten are A's. But in Japan and Germany, the A's are four in ten and O's three in ten. Experts have argued that this is one of the main reasons why we hear people say "He's typically American" or "She's typically Japanese." The French specialist Gille-Maisani even goes so far as to equate the O with what he calls "L'American way of life."

In the United States and Great Britain only about one person in ten is a B, whereas in northern India, B's make up 36 percent of the population. AB's are the rarest group. In America they are one in twenty-five. But as this book will show, AB's invariably stand out.

There are many subtle factors in blood. Your doctor might tell you that you are an A—which is all you need to know—but you might in fact belong to one of the rare A subgroups: A3, A4, A5, or the even rarer Ax, Am, Ao, AE1.

You might be RH+ or RH−. Some blood specialists believe that being RH+ strengthens your psychological characteristics, and being RH− weakens them. Extensive work on RH factors is currently in progress.

What's Your Type? is the first book to be published in the West that bridges the gap—in plain English—between the complex scientific world of hematological research and the extensive social blood group theories so popular in Japan.

CHAPTER I

THE WHO'S WHO OF BLOOD TYPES

The A Type

The main characteristic of the A type is reserved calm. In a crisis, it is the A who stays the most even-tempered and unruffled, and it is also the A who takes charge when members of other blood groups tumble into confusion.

People surrounding the A admire this deep-rooted strength, and the A often becomes the man or woman of the hour when an immediate decision has to be made, because this blood type keeps the coolest head.

A's tend to be introverts, withdrawn, even standoffish. This is a deep-down form of shyness, or vulnerability, that is stronger and more apparent in some A's, but mild and almost undetectable in others.

The A often feels nervous and ill at ease with others. But fighting against this discomfort is a powerful wish to fit in. The A wants to conform. The A wants harmony. And it is this quest for harmony that gives this group its calm exterior.

One of the driving forces behind the everyday actions of A's—something that works to their advantage, but at times also to their detriment—is a heightened sensitivity to public opinion. Who thinks what, when, and why can become overly important, and A's often find themselves more worried than they should be by questions like What does he think of me? If I do that, what will everyone say? or What will she think of me if I say . . . ?

The French psychologist Léone Bourdel points out that A's, being *"harmonique"* by disposition, owe their calmness in public to their underlying quest for social harmony. Of all the blood types, A's tend to struggle most in their pursuit of being accepted, fitting in, being loved. This is the struggle that fuels their apparent calm in dealing with people. In her book *Blood Groups and Temperaments*, she writes:

> The A is the type who adapts himself selectively, living and feeling according to a plan of constant searching for harmony with his environment. The A shows himself to be the most sensitive of all blood groups to any change in his surroundings.

In other words, the A has a natural tendency to shrink from any disagreeable rough edges that might hamper smooth social interaction.

The Chinese specialist K. H. Mee notes that in their pursuit of social harmony A's are the most polite of all the blood types, at times to the point of being overly ceremonious. A's are always trying to figure out the feelings, ideas, and dispositions of the people around them in an effort to adjust their own actions. This tendency to be polite is in fact a strategy of self-protection, of shielding the hypersensitive core of their personality.

But many A's feel that despite all their energetic endeavors they still do not quite fit in with the crowd. A's periodically find themselves thinking "Nobody understands me" or "Nobody accepts me for what I am."

Although many A's would describe themselves as socially oriented, they actually have a natural predisposition to shy away from groups and from group activity in general. In other words, they feel most secure when alone.

It is not surprising that this blood type finds itself pulled in different directions by conflicting forces. On the one hand, the A will energetically aspire to social acceptance, to taking part in group activities, but then, with equal energy, will try to steer clear of interacting with people. A's, for instance, gravitate away from team sports like baseball, basketball, or football. They typically choose solo sports like swimming, gymnastics, or long-distance running or else those in which they compete directly against another player, as in tennis or golf.

The basic quest for aloneness colors every aspect of the A's life. They are nature lovers, appreciating the solitude of a mountain hike or a walk through the fields. The A's who like living in cities do so because of the feeling of sanctuary that the anonymous crowds and buildings provides. But in general the A prefers to live in the suburbs or out in the country—far from the madding crowd. A's perceive their home, their living space, as a vehicle for isolation. The A's room is first and foremost a private refuge. The main emphasis in their houses is on the private living quarters: The bedroom is often seen as the most important part of the home, and the living room is more a place to live in than to entertain in.

One of the salient ingredients in the A's makeup is an enhanced sense of responsibility. If A's feel something should be done, they will do it. Consequently, members of this blood group are seen by their peers as being most reliable. But this sense of responsibility can also manifest itself as a feeling of guilt. A's often find themselves placing too many "shoulds" before their verbs: I should be doing this! I really should go! or I should call!

The A's also often find themselves criticized for being pessimistic, because they are not quick to adapt to new ideas or situations. Confront the average A with a new concept, and his or her first reaction will be hesitation, followed by an analysis of what's wrong with it.

But balancing the tendency to be overly careful is a deep strain of creativity. A disproportionate number of artists are A's. Below its calm exterior this group is emotional and, by extension, active in spurts—whether on canvas, on paper, rearranging the design of a room, or mixing ingredients in a recipe.

In *Character, Blood Group, and Constitution*, the Swiss specialist Dr. K. Fritz Schaer writes that A's are most energetic when they are creating something. When A's are in these phases they can move mountains—but the stream of energy is not infinite:

> The A's escalation of pace is not limitless. At some point inhibition—a slowing down—must set in. Periods of passivity are extremely important to the reactivation of this blood-type, which inevitable rebounds from this passivity, often with unexpected vigor. Then the A's vital juices flow again and life pulsates.

A potent hunger for personal accomplishment feeds the A's energy. A's are in their own way perfectionists and strongly crave success, whatever their chosen field may be. They also have a pronounced appreciation of beauty, of the harmonious, whether visual, auditory, or tactile.

A types are more tender and definitely more sensitive to art than the other blood types. The vulnerability that manifests itself in social contact resurfaces in artistic expression.

The B Type

B's tend to be rational, sober, and pragmatic—inveterate organizers. This group is the most practical blood group. It is the B type who fixes, builds, creates, who has a penchant for tinkering with machinery, and feels best when everything is running smoothly.

The members of this group are the specialists among us. They approach things with a cautious eye: They read manuals and follow recipes. When they set out to do something they spend more time than your average person on the groundwork, making notes, laying out tools. They focus intensely on what they are doing—so intensely that they will neglect everything else. This is why there is often a discrepancy between the organization of their work space and the disorder and clutter everywhere else. It is not surprising that B's are often accused of being messy.

The B's general trademark is their energetic drive to reach goals. Once a target has been set the B steers toward it with a vigor bordering at times on fanaticism. In other words, even if circumstances are not conducive, the B will doggedly push on. This group's motto: Once a course is chosen it must be followed to the bitter end.

This disposition inevitably acts as a double-edged sword. At best, it gives an attractive entrepreneurial slant to whatever the B does, which usually leads to success even when the odds are bad. But on the downside, blinkered inflexibility sometimes sets in, driving projects into the mud.

It is not surprising that B's are not the best team players. Sports like football and baseball, for instance, are particularly problematic for the B, who rebels against the structure of the team. Having to tailor strategies to other people's actions goes against the B's grain. You will find the typical B athletes in tennis, gymnastics, bodybuilding, and golf—all sports where players are responsible for their own maneuvers and stratagems.

The archetypal B's are individualists. They relate best to peers from their own blood group, not because they are particularly compatible—B's are often too individualistic for that—but because with their strongly developed sense of self they can empathize with other individualists.

The Japanese specialist Masahiko Nomi observed that because of this innate tendency to separateness, B's are volatile friends. What's on their agenda comes first. Their freedom of action, without social constraint, is important to them. B's can shock with their candor. So it is not surprising that it often takes a B to understand and appreciate a B. When not mixing among themselves, B's are most attracted to pliable individuals who are willing to follow their direction.

An interesting phenomenon is the many religious leaders who are B's. It is the B's particular predisposition to tenaciously follow things through, along with a strong attraction to doctrine and dogma, which makes members of this group perfect candidates for religious office—whatever the faith.

B's generally have a heightened sense of self, with a clear view of what they want to do and of its importance. Public opinion and questions such as What should I do? and What am I expected to do? are much less of an issue for B's than for the typical A, for instance. The B group often finds itself criticized as being self-absorbed and egocentric, even egomaniacal.

As a result, keeping schedules and dates is particularly difficult for this group. Full involvement in a project dampens the B's sense of time, added to which is the underlying notion that what has been started must be finished—an element that is more important than social reliability. So the B often stands accused of being "always late," "unreliable," and "untrust-worthy." Many B's counter by taking forceful and stringent measures to always be ten minutes early for an appointment.

The B's home is usually stocked with an abundance of functional, useful objects. Even the tidiest B's prefer living in a cluttered environment: The idea is that the B's personal things—the things he or she needs every day—must always be close at hand. In other words, the look of the B's living space is secondary to its performance capacity. Personal items in the home are chosen with more emphasis on utility than ornament.

B's often find themselves criticized for not being fun-loving, for being overdedicated to their work. They often feel ill at ease among people they don't know. Their general tendency to go their own way makes them in a sense loners—not, like the typical A, out of innate diffidence, but because deep down they prefer not to be influenced by people around them.

The B has an inveterate mistrust of sentimentality. When a problem arises, the B wants a hardheaded and matter-of-fact solution, even when the problem is personal. This tendency works well in this group's professional dealings, but often backfires in the intimate sphere of family and friends, where the B's actions can be interpreted as blunt and unfeeling.

The German psychologist Karl H. Göbber attributes the B's social qualities to their contradictory inner struggle between impulsiveness and restraint. Socially, B's are prone to blunders—mainly because they are not afraid to speak their mind. Dr. Göbber says that people are often surprised at the directness and the naïveté with which B's touch on matters that "really should not be mentioned."

Other scientists have come to similar conclusions. Dr. K. Fritz Schaer defined the B type as "reflective," with the mind controlling the emotions. Their inner lives are fueled by ideas and principles. He notes that B's are often accused by those close to them of being cold and formal, even ascetic. In *Character, Blood Group, and Constitution*, he writes, "for the B-type, the feeling of belonging to a group is not as important as it is for the A-type. The B's interpersonal relationships are generally marked by reserve, restraint, detachment, and formal comportment, along with a certain coolness."

The O Type

In the United States and Great Britain, O is the largest group—about four people in ten. The O stands out as the sociable, energetic, extroverted person who makes friends easily and has a natural tendency to mingle.

O's go with the flow and grasp at opportunities. They are more flexible than any of the other blood types, and quick to start a project or chase after an idea. But if circumstances change, O's will quickly shift gears and adapt their responses. When prospects are bad they are the first to bail out. Unlike B's, O's do not have the compulsion to follow things through at any cost. This gives everything they do a healthy and realistic touch, and their ventures are largely success-prone.

But O's are often accused of having a short attention span, of being flighty, of not thinking things out—even of being unreliable. Other blood types, especially the A's, are often surprised at the O's ability to shift focus quickly. An O might be a passionate advocate of an idea one minute and have forgotten all about it the next. O's express strong emotions in strong words, but as their interest changes they can be equally fervent about opposite ideas.

Other blood groups are often surprised by the O's candor. This group's declarations are deeply felt, but generally do not turn out to be durable or long-lasting. The feelings of the adaptable O are prone to shift—to become stronger, weaker, more complex—at a much faster pace than the feelings of other blood types. When these shifts occur, O's do not hesitate to immediately redefine their new position. As a result, they are often accused of insincerity.

O's are classic entrepreneurs. They are restless and competitive—the "active" group, as the Japanese psychologist Takeji Furukawa defines them. Their restlessness makes O's quintessential immigrants. This might explain why the percentage of O's in the United States and other nations of immigrants is higher than that in the mother countries. In Germany, France, Spain, Russia, and Poland, for instance, the A group is predominant; in India it's the B. Because blood type is hereditary, scientists have suggested that A's and B's, with their conservative, sedentary dispositions, would have resisted the upheaval of leaving their homes, preferring instead to make the best of what they had.

O's are open when it comes to expressing their emotions. You know where O's stand, what they think about you, how they feel about things. They send clear signals, and this is one reason why they interact so easily with others. Dr. K. Fritz Schaer points out that the A and B types find that they can manipulate O's because of the latter's openness and adaptability. In other words, once you have convinced an O that your idea is better, he or she is prone to agree and comply.

The O's natural tendency to sociability gives them an intrinsic elegance. They like to be noticed, and what people think is very important to them. As Masahiko Nomi points out, they have a penchant for being showy and craving attention. O's flourish in show business and the performing arts.

But the O's flexibility also has a shadowy side. Many specialists have pointed out that O's are particularly adept at crime, a notion that studies in France, Africa, and Brazil have confirmed. The O's "hyperadaptability," scientists claim, makes them particularly dexterous transgressors.

O's are dependent on their environment and seek to adapt themselves to circumstances. As a result, they keep careful tabs on anything that involves them. Words come to them easily and nimbly, whether they are at a party among friends or waiting in line at a checkout counter. Along with this natural flair for language comes a lively interest in discussion. O's like to talk out their thoughts as the thoughts arise. Self-consciousness is not a major factor in their personae. They do not hesitate to reveal their inner selves to friends and acquaintances, something the more private A would never do. This frankness never ceases to amaze the other blood groups. But O's do not share these intimate thoughts as a manifestation of closeness, but rather as a way of developing their ideas, in order to get as much input as possible from others.

O's are ambitious. Self-confidence is a strong factor in their makeup and usually acts as a spur to success. They are realists who can weigh the positive and the negative aspects of every situation.

Materialism is a strong driving force for the O. The O's home reflects the important role money and possessions play. His or her belongings are a social extension of the O's inner self. It is not surprising that the living room, specifically as a place for entertaining others, is the focal point of the O's home.

Masahiko Nomi points out that material pursuits are more important to the O than intellectual pursuits, although scientific surveys conducted by the Swiss psychologist Maurer-Groeli, among others, suggest that the O group is not intellectually weaker than the other groups.

O's do not have a natural affinity for detail. Details hold them back in their race to finish one project so that they can move on to the next. According to Dr. Göbber, O's are generalists in the sense that they are more interested in generalities than in technicalities.

The AB Type

AB's are the most intriguing of the blood types. They are laid-back and outgoing, shy and socially assertive, speculative and impetuous—a blend of striking, clashing characteristics. In the early 1930s, the Japanese psychologist Takeji Furukawa classified them as "passive." Subsequently, biopsychologists throughout the world have ranked B's and O's together as "active" in temperament, and A's and AB's as "nonactive."

AB is the rarest blood type. It is least common in the United States—about one person in twenty-five—and most common in Japan, where one person in ten is AB.

When you meet an AB, you see a calm and composed individual. The basic AB personality is one of aplomb and contemplation, and in this sense AB's are like A's. But below the surface is a fiery mix of opposites.

Unlike A's, AB's are easily triggered into action. Most people are introverted on some occasions and extroverted on others, but one disposition is dominant throughout their lives. For AB's, however, introverted and extroverted behaviors occur in almost equal measure. Of all the blood types, this group is the quickest to switch from one state to the other. It is not surprising that scientists consider AB's to be the most challenging of all the blood groups; the French psychologist Léone Bourdel even labeled them *complexe.*

AB's have a strongly developed sense of responsibility. Family and friends find them dependable and trustworthy.

They do, however, rebel when overwhelmed by other people's demands, and on these occasions they withdraw completely. Although they are very protective of their time and energy, they are prepared tó be generous, but on their own terms.

AB's are most unpredictable in social situations. At times they are taciturn: At a party they can often be seen standing alone in a corner. At other times they are the center of attention, mingling energetically. Friends and family often find themselves asking "I wonder what mood he's in today?"

AB's are unusually shy with some people and unusually bold with others. They view this reaction as a handicap, and ask themselves why, for no apparent reason, they have a phobia toward certain individuals. AB's often catch themselves engaging in social avoidance maneuvers. They might suddenly dodge across the street when they see someone they know coming, or they might look the other way and pretend to be lost in thought. People often mistake this aloofness for arrogance, and many even find it intimidating—which always surprises the AB's, who are usually aware that their apparent arrogance is nothing more than a thinly veiled form of timidity.

AB's have a strong creative strain. The *complexe* aspect of their temperament makes them inspired artists and performers—brilliant at creating and producing on all levels. Their intricate personality makes everything they do particularly compelling.

AB's are also strongly interested in metaphysics. Masahiko Nomi points out that they are drawn in surprising numbers to professions such as faith healing, fortune-telling, and astrology. In a religious sense, they are also the most spiritual of the blood groups. Many church leaders are AB's. The inherent spirituality and rationale of AB's make them successful religious figures, as does their expectation of loyalty from friends and followers. According to laboratory tests, the Shroud of Turin, which some scholars believe was used to cover the body of Jesus Christ after his Crucifixion, has specks of AB blood on it—which would make Jesus Christ the most prominent AB in history.

AB's make good politicians and diplomats. The combination of reason and flexibility in their makeup gives them the ability to handle problematic matters with quick and politic tactfulness. They are good at spotting and deflecting potentially dangerous situations. Toshitaka Nomi points to a Japanese survey which shows that a disproportionate number of Japanese mayors are AB's. But Nomi generally criticizes AB's as having a predisposition for being overly flexible; in other words, they are too good at the political game. If a situation calls for an immediate about-face, AB's are not above dropping old ideas and friends.

AB's feel comfortable in big cities because of the action, the opportunity, the interest of large crowds living in close proximity—but city life also makes them feel claustrophobic. Many AB's prefer the calm of suburbia, even a rural existence if possible. But ultimately AB's suffer under the slow-footed placidity of such a lifestyle, and AB's living in the country find themselves going in to town as often as possible. The homes of AB's reflect their restless personalities. In *Tempéraments psychobiologiques*, the French specialist Gille-Maisani defines their living spaces as a reflection of their heterogeneous— *complexe*—temperament. In his home, the AB "likes elements that inspire thought, elements that inspire action, things that are personal and things that allow communication to take place."

AB's are indeed complex: hermetic but sociable, subdued but assertive, doers and thinkers who are interested in both intellectual and material pursuits. A convergence of opposites, AB's have, in a sense, the turbulent and problematic temperament of adolescents: They are torn in too many directions, and their hardest task is centering themselves. AB's who can discipline and direct these disparate tendencies are extremely successful at whatever they do.

BLOOD TYPES AT SCHOOL

A's at School

From an early age A's want to figure things out for themselves. In their first years at school many A's already stand out as children who question what they are learning in individualistic ways—which are not necessarily the teacher's way. All children have powerful and vigorous inner lives as they struggle to make sense of the world around them. But for the A child, the processing of this information—learning—is largely a need for exploration, for imposing an order on things.

At school A's learn to control the influx of information more quickly than others, to choose what they will absorb and what they will ignore. This makes them naturally good at selecting material they feel they need out of the jumble of data they get in class. A children look at a topic broadly, see something in it that interests them, and zoom in on it, vacuuming up all the details. Teachers are often taken aback by the way their A students repackage this information.

Jake, an A journalist originally from Great Britain who now lives in the United States, talks about his ninth-grade interest in history, and his early interest in "curious angles":

> One day I was dozing as usual in my ninth-grade history class when we suddenly came to King Charles's or King Henry's marriage. I sat up with a jolt. Whatever king this was, he was marrying Princess Henrietta Maria! Henrietta was my Austrian cousin, and I immediately imagined her, plump and freckled, walking through the halls of Westminster in the same heavy, high-collared dress covered with jewels that Elizabeth I was wearing just a few pages further on in our book. Within seconds I was passionately interested in Henrietta Maria. I had to know who she was, when she was born, who her father was, her mother, and did she know any English? Within seconds I was a fanatic little Henrietta-admirer. Not that I asked the teacher any questions! I did all the research on my own. I dug up books in the library and studied for hours. On the test at the end of term there was an essay on the king's reign. I did half a paragraph on him, and two pages on Henrietta Maria. I got an A+, and the teacher, startled but impressed, said I was the only one who even remembered the Queen's name. I was a real nerd, but an unconventional one, I'd like to think.

When they are interested in something, A students have a long attention span. Like Jake, they can become quite "fanatic" in searching for information that interests them. Once their minds are set they can work happily on a project for hours at a time. But if A's are *not* interested in a subject, if they don't see its point, it is very difficult to motivate them. This is why so many A children perform erratically at school, unusually well in some subjects, and below average in others. One often hears

"He's clever, but he just won't concentrate" or "I don't know why she gets top grades in math but keeps failing in biology."

The secret for parents and teachers is to encourage A's by bringing out all the interesting and fun elements in the things that the children find dull. Because A children feel that there has to be a practical justification for learning something, it is important to present information in a clear-cut form. They prefer teachers who explain things plainly. For their own sense of security A students like to know what is expected of them in class.

Like most Japanese, Keiko, a Japanese-American mother living in New York, is very well versed in blood types. She says about her son:

> I'm an O, but both my husband and my son are A's. It's amazing how alike they are. I know how my son studies. He's in seventh grade now and hates math, and up to last year it was just F's all the way! So I stepped in. I said to him, "Come on, this is interesting stuff! It's simple. The great thing about math is that every question has only one answer—how can you go wrong? It's logical! It's fun!" We went back through the whole textbook, covered all the missing links, and before long he was convinced he was enjoying himself. And now he's getting B's and A's. I also noticed that when he writes things out neatly it makes him feel more organized, while if his book's a mess he feels lost. So I suggested he do all the arithmetic on a piece of paper first, and then copy everything neatly into his notebook. It's amazing how these little things can help.

A's learn better in a formal class setting with quiet discipline, where everyone knows what they are supposed to do. Noisy, unconventional classes spell disorganization for the A; they find this unsettling and tend to withdraw.

A children like to work on limited material so that they can build up their knowledge step by step. They need to concentrate on what they are doing, otherwise they feel they are losing control of the material.

A's prefer to work alone, a quality that characterizes them throughout their lives. Group projects like science experiments in which five or six students work together are hard for A's, since they prefer working to their own rhythm. When forced into a group, they mark out, at least symbolically, their own domain within the hierarchy—their own ground on which no one else can tread. A's are happiest when they can start, carry out, and finish things that they have begun themselves.

The A's interest in working alone is partially due to an innate resistance to change. Whether children or adults, A's prefer a stable, predictable environment. As Gille-Maisani points out, it takes A's longer than other blood groups to adjust to new classes, teachers, and classmates. Parents who move their A child to a new school should be especially sensitive to helping the child adjust to his or her new surroundings. All children try to fit new people and new pieces of information they encounter into a structure of preconceived notions. This is an important part of developing social skills. The A child tends to do this at a slower, more deliberate tempo, which is why A children can sometimes take a little longer to adapt to new environments.

B's at School

Adult B's stand out for their probing, analytic disposition. Whether artists or scientists, technicians or office workers, they like examining things from all angles, digging to the core, breaking wholes into parts. This temperament is evident from an early age. Like A's, B children prefer activities at school to be clear and organized, with information presented as logically as possible. Unlike A's, B children are more dynamic in their approach to material. They are what sociologists call *telic* learners, learners who prefer straightforward, systematized teaching that is unambiguously goal oriented. In other words, the B child doesn't like a teacher to waste time in class digressing, encouraging chaotic discussions, or presenting facts in unconventional ways. B's of all ages like order.

The B's preference for order is particularly apparent in loud, chaotic classes. High levels of external stimuli are stressful and tiring for the B's, because it makes them spend an increasing amount of energy keeping their thought patterns uninterrupted. The more boisterous the class becomes, the more the B withdraws.

B's are often slow starters at school. Early education, from preschool to about sixth grade, is largely activity oriented, with children working on projects with partners or in small groups. At this stage, learning is still often informal and loosely structured, designed to give children freedom to experiment and widen their experience. The B children in early classes are usually not quite in their element, although it is an important period for them in developing personal learning strategies. The B child finds learning much easier after the sixth grade, as the curriculum becomes increasingly formal and structured. At this point there is less emphasis on group work, and teachers encourage children to work independently. B's tend to be systematic workers with an internalized approach to learning.

B children's responsiveness to clarity and organization can be seen at all levels of learning—in school and out. They like to be presented with pragmatic information that not only makes sense, but also is applicable to what they are doing. Helen, a New Jersey truck driver in her midthirties, talks

about her early passion for machinery and how her father, a
professional mechanic, helped her learn.

> By the time I was ten, machines were all I was interested
> in. I spent as much time as possible with my father in his
> workshop. I dreamt of how I'd drive a big heavy machine
> of my own when I grew up—and, I guess, my dream's
> come true. My father never said to me, "You're a girl, what
> are you doing here?" He was never too busy to show me
> things. His work was real clean. He marked every wire,
> laid out every part, took me step by step through every
> job: "This is where you connect the transmission range
> indicator, and here are the five retaining screws you'll
> need, and that's where the negative battery cable goes!"
> By the time I was thirteen I was a real pro.

Instinctively, Helen's father was the perfect teacher for his
B daughter. He labeled pieces clearly, he demonstrated how
the different parts fit into a whole scheme, he explained why
things are installed the way they are and what their function
is. Most important, he encouraged Helen to develop her
interest, and she quickly became a specialist.

In the classroom, we see that the most successful B children
are the ones parents and teachers have encouraged to follow
their own learning patterns. Self-esteem is a powerful component of a child's learning, and B children whose seemingly
strange but usually effective work habits are constantly challenged will develop low self-esteem.

Any child with low self-evaluation is bound to do less well at
school.

Like A's, B's need stability and continuity in learning. The B
child likes to have the whole picture. If a link is missing the
B student often loses the thread and begins doing badly in
class. More than other children, B's feel they need to know

every component before they can step back and understand the whole. Changing classes or schools is particularly difficult for B's. Not, like A's, because they are apprehensive about a new environment, but because a change is an interruption, and for B's an interruption usually means a loss of perspective.

Jeffrey, a B writer in his midtwenties, speaks about an early encounter with Shakespeare:

> English Literature was my favorite subject, but I completely fell apart in eleventh grade. We moved to New York right before Christmas, and I landed in a new school after the holidays. They were halfway through *Macbeth* and I just couldn't keep up. I tried reading it on my own; I rented the video; I bought the Cliffs Notes. Nothing helped! I simply felt that there was some kind of secret in the first act that I wasn't getting, and that everything somehow hinged on this secret. Every line, as far as I was concerned, was completely out of context. Miss Brown, the teacher, was very understanding, but there was really no saving me on that one.

B's like to spend an inordinate amount of time organizing a project, preparing it, laying the groundwork. This can take the simple form of sharpening and lining up all the pencils, putting rulers, compasses, and triangles in rows, or neatly arranging and rearranging the notes on the table. Older B students sometimes spend a lot of time making notes. The B might feel *almost* ready to write his essay, but never quite ready. Luckily, the B is usually organized enough by temperament to finally write the essay and hand it in, even if it is at the eleventh hour. But in extreme cases B's spend so much time preparing that they tend not to finish projects.

But the B's natural penchant for analysis is usually a help in school. B's frequently make the brightest students, since their analytical approach to study gives them the knack for coming up with original ideas. Their logical approach gives them the edge in both science and in the humanities. B's are what some educators call *holistic* learners. They look at the whole picture, the whole subject they are studying, and examine all its aspects, reshuffling the information to arrive at a personal conclusion.

O's at School

The O's strong point at school is adaptability. Of all the blood groups, O's fit best into the structure of a class; they work productively in groups and have a natural and relaxed approach to learning.

O's are the most active and extroverted blood type. They adapt naturally to new schools and situations—they thrive on new challenges. O students need a noisy classroom, a varied teaching rhythm. Unlike their A and B classmates, they can concentrate better when a lot is going on around them, and quickly become restless, even disruptive, when things are too quiet. O students are easily motivated, but also quick to get bored. In a class that is too slow they often become jokers, teasers, or attention-getters in their need for variety. O's are what educators call *paratelic* learners: They prefer teachers who have a boisterous, unconventional approach to teaching over those who are more goal oriented.

This is true at all levels of learning. Mark, a New York hotel concierge who studied French and Spanish at Penn State University, speaks about his favorite class in O terms:

> Spanish Literature II was a mess! Professor Palsy, that's what we called her, refused point-blank to speak English. "You're Spanish majors, you have to learn the language!" She spoke the best classical Spanish; *Don Quixote* was her

model. The only problem was she had the worst Pittsburgh accent. It was a *disaster*! We had to guess half the stuff she was saying. She'd stand there in plaids and polka dots—it was the 1970s—and extemporize, swinging from El Cid to Cervantes and then back to *Lazarillo de Tormes*. She was all over the place! I couldn't wait to go to that class. It was fun, you never knew what would hit you next. She wasn't the kind of teacher who had any kind of system—but I did learn about Spanish literature, so I guess she must have been doing something right.

This class might have been problematic for the system-conscious A or B, but it worked out well for Mark, the typical extroverted O—not because of the presentation, but because the teacher managed to capture his interest.

When it comes to achieving something, O students see it as their responsibility to go for it—a mind-set they carry with them into later life. Defeatism—as in "Oh, that's too hard for me, I'm not clever enough!"—is unusual for an O. If anything, O students sometimes set their goals too high. But even when O's don't measure up to their expectations they still keep a positive attitude: "I have to try harder next time" or "I didn't study hard enough." O's don't usually see themselves as powerless pawns in the system. They have what is called an "internal locus of control," which means they take responsibility for what happens to them—a factor educators deem important for success in learning.

The O students' curiosity about new subjects and new information usually works to their advantage. While A's prefer approaching topics serialistically—a teacher starts at the beginning of a topic and builds up the information piece by piece—O's always want to hear fresh facts. But although O's scoop up information quickly, they sometimes have difficulty working deliberately toward a goal. They tend to go with the

flow, moving from one detail to the next, sometimes not stop-
ping long enough for analysis.

Keiko, an O Japanese-American New Yorker, speaks of her
interest-hopping in high school:

> I was the all-American girl, although my parents were very
> traditional Japanese. I guess when you immigrate, the cul-
> ture you didn't give a second thought to back home sud-
> denly becomes hallowed. The teachers at school pegged
> me as a total dilettante. I wanted to try everything. I did
> gymnastics for two terms—I wanted to be in the Olympics.
> Then I studied flute and wanted to play at the Met. After
> that I went for ballet—I wanted to dance with Barysh-
> nikov, and then I wanted to be a famous painter. . . . But
> when I got interested in debating I dropped everything
> else. As a matter of fact, I had a really bad conscience.
> "Keiko never finishes anything she starts!" my report card
> said. But how do you know what you're interested in when
> you're thirteen? You just have to try everything that's out
> there, right? So the debating society became my passion
> for about two years. I enjoyed it while it lasted, and it was
> good for me. I sure learned how to argue my way in and
> out of things.

Friendships at school are a very important factor in the O's
education, especially for younger O's. Their natural inclination
toward sociability and their enjoyment of group work makes
them more in tune with their environment than B students,
who are happiest working at their own rhythm. The self-esteem
of younger O's comes from their ease at mixing with their
peers. Their innate confidence gives them the security to set
high goals. O children usually stand out as the most motivated.

But O's are also unusually sensitive to peer groups—and to
peer pressure. Students in classes tend to split into different

cliques whose membership and status are in constant fluctuation. O students are quick to join, often taking charge, but they are also quick to switch if they see another clique as more prestigious. The O's peers have a direct effect on the O's attitude toward learning. O's work harder in classes where the prestigious cliques are studious. Kenneth, an interior decorator from Baltimore, talks about the strange peer pressure in his school:

> I was a total nerd in senior high. We all were nerds; it was a status thing. The idea was: Sports are out, parties are out, no drugs, no drinking, just study, study, study—"He who thinks cool is cool!" I was on the gymnastics team, but sports had such a bad image that I never spoke about it. After school we'd all meet at a diner and act like we were poets in a Paris café and talk about difficult books over cream sodas. It's embarrassing when I think about it now, but at least we read a lot of books, even if we didn't understand them.

Although the O's flexibility makes them too susceptible to outside influence, it is this very flexibility that gives them the pliancy to get ahead. O's at school—and in the workplace—always stand among the most successful.

AB's at School

AB's are the most mercurial of the blood types, a mixing of opposites: AB students are focused but at the same time scattered, methodic but inspired, scientific with artistic natures, or artistic with the precision of a scientist. They are talented in many directions and stand out in whatever they do.

But this flexibility, although a great gift, is also a challenge. Trying to decide on a project, or even on how to tackle it, can be difficult. AB's feel that there are too many leads to follow, too many interests pulling from different directions. It is hard for them to prioritize. Unlike the A's, who look at the big picture and then zoom in on the details, AB's often can't see beyond the big picture.

But AB's have an all-around curiosity and inquisitiveness that makes them good learners. AB children have a questing temperament, and often surprise their teachers by the probing questions they ask. Young AB's have a strong analytical disposition and desire for order, and their questions are often an attempt to bring order to the information that pours in on them from all sides. Boris, an AB accountant in his late twenties, talks about the barrage of questions he would ask at school:

> When I was six or seven, Disney's *Aristocats* came out and the whole class went to see it. I remember how afterward my first question threw the teacher off: "How come the mommy cat didn't jump into the river to save her kitten— I thought all mommy cats risk their lives." I knew that if I had been the cat I would have jumped in. The teacher's hesitation was a revelation to me. So she didn't know everything! The question really interested her, I could see she was trying to figure out how far a real cat would go for her kittens, how far her instincts would push her. . . . After that, there was no holding me back. Every few days I came up with a class-stopper. It always took Miss Bath by surprise, and I got a kick out of her expression as she scrambled for answers. I must have been a real joy to have in that class.

The AB child's baiting questions are often a form of what educators call *limit-testing*. School for young children is a new and radical window on life; it's the first time they regularly interact and compete with others. By testing the limits of their teachers, AB's are not just trying to figure out what they can get away with or how far they can go; they are working toward defining their surroundings and how they fit into these surroundings. Children need to learn how to perceive other people—especially people with authority—but they also have to learn how to form an opinion about them. Boris's teacher seemed to be in tune with his need for constant limit-testing and encouraged the flow of questions.

Young AB children are particularly interested in the interactions that go on in learning. When the teacher tells a story, for instance, the whole group participates. Everyone shares in the experience. For AB children this is especially important as a way for them to test and compare their reactions to those of others.

Other blood groups fit into clear molds, but AB's are hard to pin down. Unlike most students, they are both "collaborative" and "competitive" learners. On the collaborative front they work well in cadence with others—both with peers and teachers—assimilating ideas, expanding on them, and contributing their own ideas to flesh out a project. But AB's also have the edge of the competitive learner who wants to be top of the class. They can work long hours on their own, researching, studying problems from different angles, combing through their essays over and over until everything is right. This is in part a quest for originality, the need to stand out, the need to produce something special.

This AB pattern comes across in all fields of learning. Michelle, an AB ballerina, talks about her study methods as a teenager:

I realized early that the only way to make it was to stand out. It's important in whatever you do, but in ballet it is a must! I was fourteen when they came to our school to scout for new baby ballerinas. By then I was working hard on the roles I knew I was going to dance—I didn't have the slightest intention of ever being in the corps. I had it all planned. I knew that my unusual flexibility even for a dancer, my thinness, and my strong balance were all a plus, and that my weakness doing turns was a minus. So I worked hard on accentuating all the points where I could shine, and then glossed over the technical difficulties with dramatic interpretation—as in "Juliet sees Romeo, is overcome with passion, turns one and a half times on pointe, and *flies* toward him." No one had to know that I had no choice because I could barely do a clean double-turn at the time. In that run toward Romeo, I would go wild. Classmates who were much stronger did sharp triple-turns. But I was the one who was chosen for the role! Obviously my ballet master saw right through what I was doing, but he was very encouraging! He never tried to crush my little dodges—if anything, he promoted them.

Michelle is a perfect example of the successful AB student. With their complex temperament, AB's might initially have a problem centering themselves, but once they develop an effective way of marshaling their talents—getting them to work in their favor—the road to accomplishment is open. AB's have a difficult time working with conventional and autocratic teachers, because they need the freedom to develop their work at their own tempo. AB's have a personal sense of order and priority, and although their methods might seem irrational, it is important to give them the leeway to set up their own strategies. In this sense, Michelle's teacher was helpful in cultivating her personal, even idiosyncratic, approach to learning. As Michelle says, "So many teachers end up stifling their students. They tell you, 'This is how you do it—there is no other way!' I was lucky that my teacher was so open and generous in his methods."

CHAPTER III
BLOOD TYPES AT WORK

A's at Work

To function well at work the A needs logic, stability, and method. The A bricklayer lines up his bricks in a neat row before laying them; the A cook arranges all the ingredients before turning on the oven. A's feel best when their work is clearly outlined in their mind, when things make sense to them.

If their work space is in disarray, A's become nervous, even panicky. Everything has to fit a pattern, and if A's don't see a pattern they will create one. This is not to say that they are particularly tidy. Order, for the A, does not necessarily involve neatness. More often than not, the order that A's superimpose on their projects is very personal, and coworkers often stand back in amazement at their quirky work habits. The A bricklayer might need to organize his bricks in zigzag lines before laying them, while the cook might, for no apparent reason, premix some ingredients and arrange others in little mounds.

Harriet, an A homemaker from Boston in her midforties, talks about her special methods for dealing with the "grueling dinner-party schedule" she has to keep up for her husband's business entertaining:

> My kitchen is usually a disaster area—well, at least I think so. People say I'm neat, but I'm not, that's the truth! I wish I were. The only place that is really neat is the shelf where I keep my recipe books. My husband is a lawyer, so we entertain a great deal. Sometimes I have to arrange two dinner parties a week. I spend ten hours in the kitchen preparing a party, and then I have to be the perfect hostess. When I'm working, I see my kitchen almost like a chessboard, black and white squares. The dinner party starts at seven, so I just work my way through the kitchen from square to square and hope I make it in time.

However erratic the A's work methods may seem, there is always a deeper reason for A's doing things the way they do. In other words, successful A's take great care to organize their work so that they don't run aground on dangerous reefs or shoals.

A's are the most fastidious and meticulous of the blood groups. According to the Chinese specialist K. H. Mee, A's scored particularly high in carefulness on personality tests. The Japanese psychologist Y. Suzuki cites responsibility and patience as particularly strong A qualities. Toshitaka Nomi coins the phrase "the able A."

Once A's have grasped the basics of a project, they quickly move on to solving more complicated elements. In this sense they are methodical workers who successfully tackle one part of a problem at a time. But they do not work well when confronted with different problems all at once: A's do not like surprises. They feel most comfortable in a predictable environment and are uneasy in jobs that call for flexibility and quick decisions. According to the German psychologist Karl H. Göbber, "the A absorbs information carefully and with precision. He shies away from suddenness."

Toshitaka Nomi notes that A's "lack talent for instant vision, preferring the methodical careful approach that allows them to survey the terrain before putting their feet down." Among the least suitable professions for an A, Nomi lists football, public relations, and investment.

A's function well in large organizations as long as their job description is clear and defined. If it isn't, A's lose direction, and their work energy and motivation can flag. Of all the blood types, A's fit best into the hierarchy of a company. They accept direction from managers, because they have a high regard for systems and a deep faith that a group works best when everybody sticks to his or her designated role.

A's suffer from stress more than the other blood groups. When work becomes too hectic, A's have trouble dividing projects into workable units. As a result, they have difficulty coping, since they tend to internalize the stress. But A's are also good at using stress as a catalyst to goad themselves to better, sharper, more productive work habits.

The A boss is generally tough but fair. Employees who work for A's are expected to function smoothly and efficiently and be able to quickly transform ideas into practical procedures. According to the Swiss specialist, Dr. K. Fritz Schaer, the strong, almost dogmatic convictions of A's can give them a firm air of authority:

> He can influence individuals who subconsciously are wavering, who are filled with doubts and are insecure and irresolute. He frequently dominates them. At all levels of employment the A frequently ends up in leadership positions.

In general, A's make good managers but not the best leaders. They are good at developing strategies but have problems defining goals. As managers, they have a knack for organizing and budgeting, and for directing their employees' work.

The ambition of A's often propels them into high-profile jobs. But their resistance to change frequently holds them back. Temperamentally they can come across as conservative, even dogmatic. For the A, time-honored procedures are preferable to what is new and untried. "I have a whole set of hand tools that I've been working with for over twenty years," says Harold, an A carpenter from new England. "These new-fangled power tools just don't do the same kind of job. When I do an intricate cutout with a coping saw, I can feel what I'm doing, which you can't with a power jigsaw. Even if it takes longer, I have a much better feeling about the work coming straight from my hands."

A's work best in a stable, quiet environment without music, loud noises, or commotion. They cannot give 100 percent of themselves unless they are fully immersed in what they are doing. External stimuli distract these introverts and make them ill at ease. A's who have to work in noisy surround-ings become agitated and increasingly tense as the day pro-gresses. Their concentration weakens along with their work performance.

But A's rarely complain. When they face difficult situations, especially at work, they internalize their reactions. To con-front people is to create a disturbance, which is completely against their nature. The A's colleagues are rarely aware that there is a problem—usually not until it's too late: When driven to the brink, the A explodes with a vehemence that is usually out of all proportion to the seriousness of the problem.

A's devote much effort to trying to achieve balance and

harmony with their coworkers. As the French psychologist Léone Bourdel points out, the A's social interaction is *"harmonique"* across the board. What coworkers think of A's is very important to them. To function well, the A needs everyone's approval.

But in spite of all this even the most sociable A's work best alone. Their rationality makes them reliable in a work group, but they have a deeply ingrained need for their own space. When they have to work closely with others, they try at least symbolically to cordon themselves off. Their desk, their shelves, their counter space can become for them an infallible symbol of autonomy.

The A's behavior is self-conscious and meticulous in public, but quite relaxed when no one is looking. A's working alone have an easier, laid-back attitude toward what they do than A's who work with others. Toshitaka Nomi points out that the discrepancy between the public A and the private A can be quite breathtaking. He cites a Japanese insurance-company survey that identifies A's as wildly inconsistent drivers: They are by far the safest drivers when people are in the car with them, and by far the worst when driving alone.

B's at Work

B's are diligent, driven workers. Their creative ideas give them an artistic edge, but they also have a strong technical streak: B's are interested in the nuts and bolts of things, in what makes something tick. Whether B's work in science or in the arts, they are the specialists.

B's are self-motivated, with a knack for extended hours of concentrated attention, but they work best on their own ideas and projects. Going with the general flow is not their strong point, and B's who work for inflexible bosses often feel stressed and suffocated. To work well, B's need the freedom to draw up their own plans and carry them out without interference.

But despite this preference for operating alone, B's have a lot to offer in a work group. Companies find them indispensable not only because they are skillful at strategic thinking, but also because they are adept at fleshing out other people's ideas. At a meeting, the B can always be relied upon to come up with solutions to problems.

B's usually have the best ideas, but are less good at explaining them. B bosses are brilliant at telling their employees what to do, but have a hard time telling them how to do it. Aggravating this situation is that B's are often low on patience. They don't see why things that are so clear to them should be so difficult for others. Toshitaka Nomi points out that behind every successful B boss there is inevitably a good manager who does the implementing and organizing.

B's like stable environments. There is nothing more problematic than a string of conflicting orders from above, and B's can become rebellious if the orders seem counterproductive for the company. Change in general is difficult for B's, unless the change was their idea in the first place. B managers can be quite forceful in defending their standpoint at meetings, sometimes to the extent of seeming disruptive. But B's tend to like conflict; not in the negative sense, but in the sense that when they clash with others, the resulting struggles can have positive results. B's with a strong managerial background are often masters at managing and manipulating conflicts. In *Blood Groups and Managerial Style*, Dr. Yungnane Yang defines the B's work methods as analytical: The B "has a high tolerance for ambiguity and is oriented to task and technical concerns."

Public opinion is low on the B's agenda. Who thinks what at work is usually of no importance to them; as a result, they often come across as gruff and overly self-assured. They don't stand on ceremony, and coworkers who are not used to their ways can find them overaggressive and intimidating.

As Helen, a B truck driver from New Jersey, says:

> I've always been into cars and trucks since I was a little girl. My dad was a mechanic. My mother would dress me in frilly things, but day after day I'd be with my dad in his garage helping him put in fuel injectors, adjusting belt tension, playing with bleed valves and brake hoses. I know my engines OK, but guys are always surprised I can even unscrew the gas cap. I don't take no shit from no one when it comes to my engines. I just do my own work. I grew up in a garage—I can take a truck engine apart and put it together again in a couple of hours, and I do.

B's always go their own way. They know their work and follow it through with confidence, seeking others' help only when they absolutely need it. In *Tempéraments psychobiologiques*, Gille-Maisani relates this reluctance to ask for assistance to the B's "independence from the environment." B's are not as strongly affected as other blood types by what happens around them; this is true on both a physical and an interpersonal level. For instance, B's are not as influenced by cold, heat, or bright lights as an O or an A would be, nor do they react as intensely to what their colleagues do or say.

Gille-Maisani warns that this independence from the environment can lead to a reckless approach to work. He cites the example of Peter the Great's decision to build St. Petersburg in a marsh "on the basis of a political idea" and then following through with the project, even as it became increasingly costly and impracticable. Peter the Great said he would build the city, and he built it.

Despite the dangers, this single-mindedness makes B's among the most successful individuals in the world. In a modern company setting we see B's "independence from the environment" translate into self-esteem that encourages them to set higher goals than those of the average worker.

The work habits of B's are governed by two completely opposing forces. On the one hand, B's are motivated self-starters who prefer to be left to their own devices, but on the other they are attracted to regulations, what Masahiko Nomi calls "ready truths." B's will say, "We have to do it! It's company policy!" or "The *employees' handbook* says you must do it this way!"

Even if a situation requires flexibility, the B often prefers to stick to the rules. Of all the blood groups, B's are hardest to pin down between conservative dogma and creative rebellion.

The B's attraction to ready formulas also makes them the group most suitable for mechanical, repetitive tasks. They are more comfortable than others in a conveyor-belt job, where they can slip into autopilot. Dr. K. Fritz Schaer says that the B "moves steadily toward his goal, more interested in the past and the future than in the present."

The fact that B's are less interested in the "now" makes them particularly good at tedious jobs. They can simply turn off their nine-to-five experiences and focus on the evening or the weekend. When things get particularly difficult they invent incentives for themselves, often simple things such as a cappuccino on the way home, a movie, or wine with dinner.

O's at Work

O's thrive on action. They are outgoing and people oriented, go-getters who are quick to seize opportunities. O is the largest blood group in the United States, and international biopsychologists have suggested that the numerical supremacy of American O's is the source of the national flavor of enterprise and venture in the United States—

"L'American way of life," as Gille-Maisani calls it. No nation in the world, he says, can quite match the American touch for *"le business"*:

> The American way of life embodies [the O's] psycho-biological temperament: predominant extroversion, quick optimism, the priority given to adaptability and social values (the importance of personal relations, expertise in organization, team sports), a society that is fundamentally democratic (the boss seen as a coordinator), and competition based on money—*le business*. It is surely no accident that the Americans' technological and scientific superiority is due as much to their flair for organization as to their creativity.

O's—American or otherwise—are quintessential team players. They need movement, interaction, and constant input from others. Solitary jobs are particularly difficult for the O: O writers, painters, night watchmen, and agricultural workers have a hard time spending long hours working alone. When O's land in such professions they usually balance the scales by rushing out after work to mix with as many people as they can. We see the O writer barhopping, the O painter on wild party rounds, the O farmer driving into town every evening.

O's prefer gregarious jobs in sales, marketing, and banking. In the arts they prefer to work in groups, in theater and ballet companies, for instance; as long as there is teamwork, the O thrives.

Raphael, an O literary agent, says that it is the "co" aspect of coworking that really provides him with job satisfaction:

> When I put a manuscript on the market and it makes the rounds of publishers, sparks fly. The editors and I

are the best of friends! But when the auctioning starts we become sharks. We smile, we negotiate, we drink cocktails, they invite me for lunch, I invite them for lunch. Network, network, network! We wheel and deal, bounce off each other, and in the end, well, the best man or woman wins. All's fair in love and publishing, you know!

A's and B's are often amazed at the O's work habits. O's like being challenged to the maximum, so much so that many actually relish the stress that comes with work overload. But while they enjoy taking on more than they can handle, this trait can also turn against them. O's forge ahead to get as much done as quickly as possible and have no time for details. In the rush, important things can fall through the cracks: O's lack the precision of the A or the tenacity of the B. What also surprises coworkers from other blood groups is the O's preference for working in a loud, preferably music-filled environment. Lock an O alone in a soundproof office and by the end of the day he or she will be climbing the walls.

From the moment O's join an organization they stand out as experts at handling peers and bosses. At the initial interview O's come across as self-confident, with good communication skills. Once hired, they acclimatize with ease, unlike the A, for instance, who needs a long initial period of adjustment. Most O's are especially good at networking. As they settle in, they use their social skills to grasp at any opportunity for promotion. Their motto is: "If I fit in well, I'll do well."

Keiko, a Japanese-American who works for the human resources department in a large New York hotel, says that she can always spot the O at an interview:

I'm an O, and I swear I can always pick out another O the moment he or she walks into the room. It's the energy.

We O's, we're just out there, ready to attack a job. It's a good quality! I'm American, although my background is Japanese. My family's from Japan, and there everyone really knows blood group psychology. There are thousands of books on it, and magazines print stuff every week. You even get hired depending on your blood group. The company will say things like "We have three B's already in that department, let's get an O." . . . When any of us here in human resources are considering someone for a job, personality is the most important factor. We grade applicants according to particular traits like their energy, assertiveness, initiative, determination, confidence, and so on. The O always scores high in these things. Of course, you always have to be careful of what our handbooks call "similarity error." That's when you prefer someone who's like you. So even though I can guess that an applicant must be an O like me, I'm always careful not to just say, "OK, you're hired!"

O's have high self-esteem, which helps them set and achieve goals at work. They have a strong sense that their environment, and what happens to them in it, is their responsibility. Sociologists define this as having a high *internal locus of control.* In other words, O's see themselves as accountable for how their careers unfold, and do not hold fate, coworkers, or bosses responsible. As a result, O's prefer to influence others rather than to respond to influence. This strategy generally works to their advantage, but often O's lose out because they are so focused on reaching a goal that they neglect to do their homework. O's need constant change and stimulation: Sometimes they face the problem of not being able to sit still in one place long enough to get something done.

The job has to be interesting and the money good, but if the O has to choose between the two, money will usually win.

Money equals success for the O, and job fulfillment comes second. This choice colors the O's need for achievement, which is as strong as that of the most ambitious B's, but the O's need is fueled more by social questions than just love of work: "Do the others think I'm successful? How do they see me? Am I achieving my goals?"

The O's strongest point is not the technical aspects of their work, the nitty-gritty of the trade, but their ability to deal with people. This sometimes gives them the unfortunate image of being competent, but not always reliable.

Even though O's are unbuttoned bosses, willing to accommodate change, who's who in the company is important to them. As they move up the organizational ladder, their managerial style often relies increasingly on their social skills. They present their ideas forcefully, but their general attitude is "Don't bother me with the details!"

According to Toshitaka Nomi, "the O boss always sets his sight on the results. Unfortunately, this sometimes means that he pays too little attention to how the job gets done or to the problems associated with getting the job done."

AB's at Work

In the 1960s, Léone Bourdel called AB's *complexe*. Throughout the world they are the rarest of the blood groups: about one in twenty-five in the United States, Canada, and Germany, one in thirty in Great Britain, France, and Spain. But they definitely stand out. In every organization they are the people everyone notices, those with remarkable potential. They have the systematizing temperament of the A, the drive and precision of the B, and the suave sociability of the O. They are creative, they are technicians, and they are fanatic specialists, but they are also given to wild generalizations.

AB's are an interesting melting pot of talent and temperament; this can push them to the top of their professions or completely derail them.

The outstanding feature of the AB's career is the urge to job-hop. It is a type of restlessness, a feeling that they are missing something by staying put: "Work is dull here, I could do better somewhere else."

Michelle, an AB ballerina, describes herself in typical AB terms:

> In the ballet world people tend to move from one company to the next, fishing for better contracts. I've taken it to the extreme. Looking back, I've never spent more than two seasons with the same company. But you know, it's turned out to be a good thing. In two years I company-hopped my way from the corps de ballet to principal dancer, and now I only go for the best roles— Giselle, Coppélia, Juliet. If you have the kind of stamina to start from the beginning over and over again, it can really work for you: You just go after what you feel is best for you.

Working on a role, Michelle has the calm, organized approach of the AB. While her colleagues often throw themselves into a project full force, taking risks as they "lunge their way into a character," she likes to approach a role carefully, to "build it up from nothing."

> Other dancers look at their roles and then zero in. But I guess my temperament makes me go really slow. It's more a fear of bungling than anything else, really. Say I'm dancing Juliet. I don't just become Juliet overnight; I work my way into her character inch by inch. The secret is that I'm quite passionate inside and I just

have to keep things in check when I'm working. If I don't, I'm lost.

The complex nature of AB's makes them cautious workers. Toshitaka Nomi says that they are unusually indecisive: "Often, an early lesson in the fact that they cannot choose will automatically steer them away from situations and jobs where decisions need to be made." Whatever their place in an organization, AB's feel that they have to repress their many-sided temperament if they are going to get anything done, especially when working in a group. In an office position, for instance, the AB will take extra steps to strictly systematize everything—papers, pencils, files—"to keep things in check," as Michelle puts it. AB's who don't take these precautions fall victim to disorder. Work begins to pile up, and they spend most of their time sifting through the jumble. Notwithstanding the AB's calm exterior, when job stress sets in their cool image can crack: AB's can only be pushed so far before they explode.

This need for a system also spills over into their view of how an organization should be set up. On the one hand, their volatile temperament urges them toward innovative change, but they generally feel more comfortable within a defined structure. In their internal quest to keep everything clean and systematic, AB's can become overly authoritarian in their views. The traditional values of the workplace in some cases become overbearing, and obeying power—blindly if need be—can take on a central importance.

AB's are generally unpredictable. This makes them interesting and creative, always ready to come up with surprising results. At a company meeting it is the AB who can be relied upon for idiosyncratic but effective solutions. But AB's also have a dogmatic strain. They feel somewhat threatened by their environment and are happy to see others follow ideas that they put forward. AB's are unsettled by disputes in the workplace, even when these disputes are based on differences that can lead to advantageous changes.

The AB's lack of ease with their environment also gives them a naturally sharp eye for trouble. They are good at scanning a group for hidden problems, at reading where other employees stand. AB's in charge are keen troubleshooters, quick to identify issues and address them.

John, an AB professor in his midforties, is chairman of his college department. He discusses what he calls his "sixth sense" when he presides at departmental meetings:

> With the increasing budget cuts in education, meetings at the university can be quite contentious. . . . My function as department chairman is to get people to calm down and look at problems as rationally as possible under the circumstances. Colleagues have often expressed surprise at what you could call my sixth sense at spotting who will flip their lid, when, and under what circumstances. It's important to keep everyone interacting smoothly.

As bosses, AB's are good at differentiating themselves from other employees while managing to keep in close touch with them. AB's have a feel for effective leadership and management—they get people to do things. When negotiating with employees working for them, for instance, they tend to avoid the forceful, don't-ask-me-any-questions approach of demanding that things be done. They prefer to negotiate.

Yet AB's also tend to have mood swings when under pressure, which can make people working for them wary. Often the consensus is "Careful, you never know when the boss might explode."

Despite the AB's tendency toward volatility, if they do manage to channel their many good qualities they go straight to the top. According to Toshitaka Nomi, "As long as there is a master plan, a clearly defined goal, a company could not do better than to choose an AB to effectively execute an initiative."

CHAPTER IV

BLOOD TYPES AND INTIMACY

The Intimate A

The A is not the type to tumble easily into a new friendship. A's initially act cool with strangers. They can seem unapproachable, and their natural shyness in public makes them appear abrupt to people who don't know them. As a result, finding a partner, especially the right partner, is difficult for the A, who often lacks the temperament for grabbing opportunities, for establishing the initial contact with a person that can lead to friendship, intimacy, and love.

A's often envy O's and AB's who mix so easily, who always seem to know what to say, how to start a conversation, how to keep people listening and responding. Socializing does not come naturally to A's. When surrounded by people—especially people they don't know—they feel besieged, and the mixing and mingling that other blood groups enjoy so much is more like hard work for them. After a long party the A wants to get away, to spend time alone, almost as if to refuel, to tank up on energy. The A's circle of friends is small and select, and consequently it usually takes the single A a long time to meet a partner.

In *Blood Group and Type*, Dr. Karl H. Göbber writes:

> The A's reserve and timidity keep him from exposing his emotional life to the curiosity of others—he believes that a person's innermost feelings should not be displayed. The A only comes alive when he is among close friends. He feels that they are extensions of himself and freely reveals his emotions. In a crowd of people he sees himself as forsaken and lonely. He suffers from being so serious and aloof. He feels that it is something that fate has inflicted on him, which, hard though it is to bear, makes him stand apart.

Jake, an A journalist living in New York, complains that he is a skilled mixer in a work setting, but shy and inhibited at parties. As a journalist, he has learned to be outgoing on the job, quick at throwing questions and following hot leads, but outside the work setting, as a private person, Jake often feels insecure:

> At parties I stand there trying to look cool and with it. My friends who know me from work think I'm really on the money, but drop me in a room full of people I don't know, and I panic. I just *can't* walk up to someone and start talking—especially not to a woman. No way! I guess I'm shy. But the thing is, I'm not always shy. If I'm standing there and she walks up to me and takes the initiative, then everything is OK. Then I'm sharp, cool, witty. But that hardly ever happens. Or, say, if I'm introduced to a woman and she's warm and interesting, and she's my

type, then there's really no problem. It's always that first step that I simply can't get myself to take.

Like most A's, Jake's *communication apprehension*—his nervousness during social interaction—is most pronounced in a casual, relaxed environment: "When I can't hide behind my ironclad role as the hard-driving journalist."

Outside the workplace, the structured environment they know and feel comfortable in, the A's first step toward a person might seem hard, almost impossible. But once an A makes contact, things loosen up.

In a one-on-one situation A's are in their element. They are what social psychologists call *dyadic*—happiest when they can relate directly to one person, instead of to many people at once. Despite their profound shyness, A's are avid *intimacy seekers*. Regardless of how aloof they may seem, the single A man or woman wants to meet a person with whom they can bond.

At the beginning of a relationship, this intimacy-seeking tendency turns into the A's strongest point. Right from the start they are focused on the person they are interested in. While the more convivial O might come across as an appealing social butterfly, A's are quickly capable of centering their attention on a person and communicating sincerely with him or her. As a result, although many specialists—Schaer, Bourdel, Gille-Maisani, Mee—point to A's as the least personable of the blood groups, they are the group most open to a deep relationship.

Closeness between two people is built on a foundation of trust and knowledge—you can't feel close to someone you don't know. The first step toward intimacy is self-disclosure: explaining who you are, revealing private details, snippets of information about yourself. A's do this naturally with someone they like. They have a deep affinity for conceptual thinking and personal feelings, and as a result are much more in touch with what is happening inside them than other blood types. A's tend to be introverted, spending a great deal of time in introspective thought and soul-searching. Because they know themselves better and are more interested in themselves and their emotions, they can disclose themselves more profoundly than their more extroverted friends. In *The Transparent Self,* Jourard writes that speaking intimately about oneself is good for developing one's own perspective of who one is—an important element in a strong relationship: "When a person has been able to disclose himself utterly to another person, he learns how to increase his contact with his real self, and he may then be better able to direct his destiny on the basis of this knowledge."

Intimacy comes both in word and in action. Beyond the things that are said are the signs and symbols lovers exchange: long gazes, touching, smiling. The intimate A is what is called in the field a *touch-approacher,* someone who revels not only in physical contact with the loved one, but who tries to communicate on all levels as intensely as possible—to merge with that person.

Friends are often surprised at the difference between the workaday A and the intimate A. In routine, everyday situations A's are actually *touch-avoidant.* They don't like being touched, they find eye contact with strangers unnerving, and they lean back—sometimes even only an inch or two—when people come too close. Not so the intimate A.

Keiko, a Japanese-American O married to an A, talks about her husband's two conflicting sides:

> My husband Jeremy is an A, and like all A's he's got two sides to him: the cold and businesslike one at the office, and the warm, gentle one that only I know. We met at the hotel where we worked. He was in corporate sales at

the time, and I was in human resources. My first impression: attractive, very handsome, but intimidating! I was almost scared of him—it was like I almost thought he hated me or something. But boy was I wrong! We got to talking at the Christmas party, and within minutes I knew he was the man for me. . . . I'd say it was love at first sight, but we had been nodding coldly at each other at the hotel for years.

At their first real meeting Jeremy demonstrated his interest in Keiko by providing all the necessary intimacy triggers that are sent out like subtle probes to communicate one's intentions and scout what the other person's intentions are. Speaking his first words to Keiko was hard for Jeremy, but when he did, he came across as sensitive and sincere, and Keiko opened up to him. His frankness and his readiness to disclose himself to her gave her the feeling that he might be the kind of person she could be intimate with.

The Intimate B

B's are individualists: They like to do things their way and are happiest when a partner follows their lead. Even in the most intimate circumstances B's wade in with a rational, straightforward stride. This clarity of approach makes them the most misunderstood of the blood types. They are often showered with complaints like "Why are you so cold to me?" "You're always so practical!" or "Even if you don't have anything to say, you could still call!" B's have a strong sense of the importance of what they undertake, and consequently often miss out on the small, delicate demonstrations of affection that reassure their partner of their commitment. The extreme B's, for instance, might wonder why they have to keep saying "I love you": "Isn't once enough?" they ask.

But this slightly perilous practicality also serves as an effective cornerstone for intimacy. The B's dedication to what they do spills over into their relationships. Dr. K. Fritz Schaer notes that B's are "possessed by the idea of duty and work." Once they have decided to commit themselves to something or someone, they see it as their duty to follow through to the end.

In this sense, B's have both a high *intimacy motivation* and a high *intimacy capacity*. They regularly ask themselves what they need to do to keep a bond with their partners going. Intimacy involves stripping away the layers of protective defenses to reveal the true feelings and susceptibilities in a relationship, and B's go for this with method and vigor. When there is a problem in the air, they are ready to reveal all and to talk about emotions such as hurt feelings, fear, and anger. If they see that they are the origin of a problem, and that it is they who must change their behavior, they do so without hesitation. As Gille-Maisani writes in *Tempéraments psychobiologiques*: "Decisively active, the B likes things to move, and is quick to take action. . . . His judgement is objective, critical; he scorns sentimentality."

The practical B's motto is: If it makes sense, then I'm for it!

Helen, a B from New Jersey in her midthirties, talks about the rough start of her relationship, which almost led her to break up with her A fiancé, Bob:

> Six months after we met, Bob almost walked out on me. I was devastated. I thought we'd been doing so well. But he accused me of being distant, cold, of not loving him. He had tried to talk to me before, but I thought he was just being oversensitive. When he finally said "That's it!" I was amazed at how unhappy he had been. It had never occurred to me that he thought I was cruel. Sometimes I

was too busy to answer his calls; I felt I needed my space, so I wouldn't always sleep over at his house; I only said I loved him once, maybe twice, and then only because he forced me to—after all, I thought my actions spoke for themselves! When the crisis came, I suddenly saw that what I was doing hurt him. It was obvious Bob needed me to be more open and gentle, and because I love him it was the easiest thing to do. . . . So now I say "I love you," I don't just think it. And I try to show him that I do in many small ways. When I'm out working and I think of him, I'll call just to tell him I miss him.

Like A's, B's are natural *self-disclosers*, ready to share who they are, what they think, what their feelings are. But while A's do this more spontaneously, B's sometimes have to be prodded. They are highly goal-oriented individuals and often are too centered on whatever they happen to be doing at a given moment to be aware that their partners feel neglected. But once they realize what is happening, they quickly confront the problem with their full attention. In intimacy, B's have a strong capacity for *self-actualization*—for striving toward bettering themselves within their relationship. As in Helen's case, when they realize what is happening, B's will gladly do an immediate about-turn to solidify their relationships. Once you see through the rugged protective covering, the B is revealed as a thoughtful and dependable lover.

In an intimate relationship, B's show the same pattern of confiding as A's. They are eager to share their thoughts and feelings in an attempt to maintain and further the intimacy with their partners, and their inherently rational temperament gives them the tools to formulate their ideas clearly. There is often a large gap between feeling that you *can* confide in someone you love and actually confiding in him or her. The B usually goes all the way, convinced that frankness and truthfulness are vital in a relationship. B's sometimes take this to tactless extremes. If something is the way it is, the B doesn't see why it shouldn't be disclosed. The partner might have a weight problem, and the B will candidly say that she prefers slimmer men, and wouldn't it be great if he could lose one or two of those tires. The B might say he's always found very tall women attractive, even though his partner is only five-two—it is the truth, after all, and by saying this he doesn't mean that he loves her less. When it comes to details like this, B's are often surprised at the resulting "overreaction" of their partners.

In relationships where both partners are B's, the plain-spoken commentary can have a rattling effect. Andrew and Lyn, a married couple in their late thirties and both B's, speak of how their constant well-meaning fashion-counseling finally brought them to loggerheads:

One day, after a big fight, my wife and I realized that we were constantly criticizing each other's looks. We're both quite vain, so it was *seriously* getting on our nerves! She'd tell me I looked tired . . . was I OK? . . . that the barber cut my hair too short, what a big pity! Then my hair was getting long and scraggly, and what were those tiny little pimples, was it something I was eating? Those jeans without that belt looked awful. This would go on and on—she works in fashion, and felt she was giving me professional advice, and I guess she was. In the meantime, I wasn't acting any better myself—not to pay her back or anything, I just thought *I* was being helpful. I'd be saying things like "Your body was so beautiful when you were a dancer, you should cut back on eating all that fat—it's the Brie, that's what's doing it!" or "No, honey, don't wear those pants, they make your butt look too big!" After our fight things have changed. Since we're both sensitive about our looks, we've cut back on the criticism. Anyway, we *do* find each other attractive.

Despite a mild case of recurring tactlessness, B's are the best of all the blood groups at maintaining intimacy over the long run. Once a partner knows that the B's periodic coldness is part of his or her temperamental makeup and not an indication of lack of interest, the intimate bond is likely to remain stable and lasting.

What B's sometimes lack in empathy, they make up for in their *perspective-taking* capacity. Once they turn their attention on a problem they will attempt to look at it from all angles. Initially, the partner might interpret a seeming lack of sympathy or support in a moment of need as proof that deep down the B is indifferent to him or her. But what is usually happening is that B's, who naturally tend to tackle things one by one, can be slow to react when they are concentrating on something else.

The Intimate O

The O, the most sociable of the blood types, surprisingly has the hardest time finding the right person to be intimate with. The O is outgoing, energetic, generally pleasant to be around. And yet, at the end of the day, single O's often complain that despite their many good friends, the parties, the fun, they are the lonely ones.

Recent psychological research points to the fact that individuals with the most developed social competence and interpersonal skills are not necessarily the best at establishing intimate contact with another person. This is particularly true of the gregarious O, who is more at ease interacting with many people simultaneously than singling out the one special person. Average O's are not *intimacy-motivated*. When single A's feel that they could do better at finding a soul mate if only they had the O's suave sociability, they don't realize that they themselves are often ahead of the game because of their dyadic nature; because of their ingrained anxiety in crowds they are happiest when interacting with just one person.

Surrounded by people at a party, the quintessential O subconsciously feels ill at ease if he or she spends too much time alone with one other person. If O's are monopolized by someone who finds them interesting or attractive, they begin to feel uneasy, even if that person intrigues them. Who knows who might be just around the corner by the buffet, or over there by the bar? More fun people! O's must get there, or they might miss out. The extreme O wants to meet everyone. Unlike single A's, single O's don't usually think of social interaction as a potential way to fulfill their need for intimacy.

Mark, an O New Yorker who works as a hotel concierge, talks about his difficulty in establishing intimacy despite his extremely sociable, outgoing nature:

> Many of my friends won't go to a party unless they know people there—not me! If I go to a party, I want to meet as many new people as I can. I often find myself cutting short a conversation with someone because I feel I'm spending too much time with them. I need to mix and mingle. If I find someone interesting, I tell myself I can always come back later and pick up where we left off. Although, with so many people to meet, I guess I often don't get back. When I see a group I don't know I head over and jump right into the conversation. I enjoy being the center of attention; I tell people jokes and stories. Everyone crowds round, everyone wants to get to know me, it's great! My big problem has always been that with so many people out there I don't seem to be able to make

contact with just one person. It's not that I don't try, but here I am, thirty-four, a good catch, and still single.

But if O's are really interested in someone, their social suppleness can save the day. While an AB might not be able to work up the courage to approach the person they find so attractive, O's feel much more comfortable taking the initiative. Their heightened skills of social interaction—and their years of practice at it—make them particularly sensitive and responsive to the intimacy signals the other person sends out. If the person seems reserved, the O knows to approach with care; if the person is outgoing, the O approaches more boisterously. In these situations O's become social superdiplomats.

In *Tempéraments psychobiologiques*, Gille-Maisani stresses that O's have a strong ability to look at a situation from many sides at once: "The O hardly ever jumps to conclusions, but pays great attention to circumstances; he seeks to resolve problems by conciliation. He extols the freedom of contact and interaction."

People tend to talk to prospective partners about what interests them most. As typical extroverts, O's are generally outward-looking: Their main interest when they are with a person they find attractive is to make that person talk about himself or herself, so that they can get to know the person. The O comes across as genuinely interested in others, and this can be an effective intimacy trigger. O's are also *touch-approachers*—they enjoy close proximity and respond positively to physical contact, which in the early stages of intimacy sends the signal that they are personable, positive, and gentle.

The extroverted nature of the O brings with it a heightened capacity for empathy. As O's are more interested in what their partners are thinking or doing than in what is going on inside themselves, they are also more likely to express compassion and concern when the other person has a problem. While a B, for instance, might need extra time to sense that something is wrong, the O is quick on the uptake. O's have enhanced communication skills, and consequently are good at expressing their understanding and support for their partner.

O's find their interpersonal skills particularly useful in the first stages of intimacy. They have a natural ability to assess the other person's attitude toward them as they begin "decoding" the other's personality, answering questions like "Is he right for me?" "Do we have enough in common?" "Is she interested in taking this further?" O's are expert readers of inadvertent signs and signals, the *indirect disclosures* people send out.

Keiko, a Japanese-American O, says that the first few minutes of conversation with Jeremy, who later became her husband, made it clear he was the right man for her:

> The first thing he told me was that he was studying Mohawk, you know, the language, which really caught me off guard. I thought, "This is amazing! This man is so interesting! Mohawk, wow, that's original! I mean Spanish, French, OK, but Mohawk?" He was shy, but I could tell he was as attracted to me as I was to him. He wanted to impress me, and I made it clear that I was impressed! I mean, here he was, this tall, attractive man from Philadelphia who was learning Mohawk. So I got him talking about it and my interest loosened his tongue. I had read somewhere that Mohawk has very long words like *thing-of-metal-in-which-wood-is-burnt-to-cook-the-things-we-eat* for "oven." So I said something like I wondered whether the length of the words reflected a special Mohawk approach to time. It sounds inane, I know, but it sure got him thinking.

Psychological studies have shown that it is men who usually prompt women to disclose information during *compatibility-*

testing in a preintimacy situation. In Keiko's case, she, as the extroverted O, took the initiative. In their first conversation, Keiko, in classic O fashion, amassed a string of useful data that assured her that Jeremy and she were compatible—that he was the right person for her to be intimate with. As she skillfully maneuvered this conversation she was strategically probing his personality, making it clear that she was interested in him.

The Intimate AB

With their complex temperament, AB's are the most intriguing blood type in intimacy. The difficulty of pinning them down, of guessing their next move in a relationship, makes them a challenge to be with—in both favorable and unsettling ways. In *Tempéraments psychobiologiques*, Gille-Maisani classifies AB's as "HMR"—*harmonique-mélodique-rythmique*—a label that captures the scope of their mercurial temperament.

Prospective partners find AB's compelling from the first few moments they spend with them. AB's come across as unusual, asking remarkable questions, discussing things from surprising angles. When AB's are interested in a person, they have a knack of making him or her feel comfortable, even if the questions and self-disclosures might be putting the other person on the spot. Harriet, a Bostonian A, remembers an intense first meeting of this kind with her AB husband:

I met my husband at a Red Cross benefit in 1971. I remember the day well. He came up to me and I was riveted—I couldn't move, I couldn't speak. He asked questions, and I answered. It was so intense. In the middle of it all he told me he wanted me to come to his place— to see his etchings, believe it or not—so I put down my champagne glass and left with him before we were even called in for dinner. I had never done that before with anyone, and to this day I can't believe it happened that way.

Emotional intensity, an important part of intimacy, comes naturally to AB's, and they inspire this intensity in others, too. In budding relationships, AB's are masterful string-pullers. Intimacy between two people is extremely complex and needs careful directing, and AB's, with their sensitive, turbulent inner lives, are good at crafting and monitoring a developing relationship.

In a crisis, AB's have a particularly strong capacity for objectivity. They can read through the outer layers of what the other person does and says, and consequently are not as hurt as other blood types sometimes are by a partner's seeming coldness or abruptness.

Instead of seeing an outburst as a symbol that the relationship is not working, or that the partner is generally conflictive, the AB will try to figure out what the problem is.

As the most flexible of the blood types, AB's are also the most adept at adjusting their behavior to the needs of the other person. They try to learn and better themselves as their relationships unfold, subtly modifying their personae. They might sense that their partners need them to be more open about why they do things, or to be more verbal about their feelings, or simply to be more tender. Once the AB's have assessed a problem, they are quicker than others at modifying their ways.

AB's accept their partners as they are. In other words, they don't try to change them to conform to a preconceived image. But while AB's encourage independence, they also require their own space. Even in the most intimate relationships, AB's keep up their guard, feeling that they need to

maintain some separation, no matter how intense and intimate the relationship might be. This helps them organize
their complicated temperament—their *"complexe"* nature, as
the French specialists call it.

The delicate protective fence that AB's build around themselves often induces their partners to have idealized notions
of them. AB's manage quite unintentionally to keep a strong
element of mystery in their relationships. We see the lawyer
who perceives his AB journalist wife as working in an
intriguing and obscure area outside his jurisdiction, or the
AB writer's wife to whom her husband's writing is an elevated,
almost metaphysical aspect of his persona that she has no
access to.

Michelle, an AB ballerina, says that her concentrated work
in the ballet world, a world to which her husband has no
access, serves as a catalyst to their intimacy:

> I have always been clear about needing my space. I
> married young; I was still in my teens. It's been over ten
> years now, but my husband understands that I have two
> clearly separate lives: my life in the ballet world, and
> my life with him. On many days I spend eight, nine, even
> ten hours rehearsing and performing at the theater—
> and he is in no way involved in what I do there. He'll
> come to premieres and galas and benefit dinners, but
> that's it. After dancing all day I'm happy to escape from
> it all and be close to him. I look forward to coming home
> to him; sometimes on a bad ballet day he's my only
> beacon of light! We almost always eat out. I like a glass or
> two of good red wine. After all these years, it's almost as if
> we've just met and we're dating. I think that if you can't
> spend as much time as you want with the person you love,
> then the time you can spend with him becomes very
> special.

The AB's aspiration for space often helps keep intimacy fresh and new. But AB's also find themselves accused of being secretive, of withholding themselves.

In intimacy, there is a thin line between a positive amount of separateness and what psychologists call *distance*—when a partner takes specific measures to obstruct intimacy. AB's sometimes have a hard time telling the two apart. Often, especially when AB's are under stress, they find that they set up a thick-walled barrier around themselves. They do this not only to protect themselves, but also to have the space they need to work things out. This is often the basic source of friction in relationships where one of the partners is an AB: The AB becomes overly preoccupied, usually about work, withdraws, and becomes distant and cold. The partner sees this retreat as having to do with the relationship and confronts the AB— and the AB withdraws further.

Marty, Michelle's B husband, says that their early relationship was rocky until he realized that her work-related anxiety sometimes made her tense, and that he wasn't understanding and supportive enough when she needed him to be:

> At the beginning of our relationship we used to fight a lot. There were times when Michelle would come back from rehearsal in an absolutely foul mood. For half an hour or so I wouldn't notice anything, but then things would start deteriorating. This could last for a couple of days. She'd be cold, hardly speak to me, and I'd think to myself, "Well, this is it!" I'd get really depressed, and even start considering divorce—don't tell her this! Now, after all these years, I know that her occasional periods of withdrawing are her way of working out her own problems. There are just times when she needs her space. So now I make a point of being very supportive when she is like that, even if I feel I have my own problems that need

taking care of. Since we've done this, I couldn't wish for a better relationship.

All relationships between two people, from casual friendships to solid marriages, are fluid and complex and have to be carefully crafted and managed. AB's might not be the easiest partners to handle because of their complexity, but they are the most prone to use all their inner resources to make things work.

CHAPTER V
BLOOD TYPES
AND MARRIAGE

The Married A

Married A's are *metacommunicators*. They like to talk things through, not just to talk. In a crisis they try to pinpoint the causes behind a problem, and once they determine a cause, they want to explore options that might lead to a solution. In an argument, A's tend to seek common ground instead of arguing about the actual issue. A's usually manage to avoid the dangerous habit of simply focusing on the crisis alone: They search hard for what might lie behind it. The A will say, "We're not communicating! Why?" not, "We're not communicating! It's your fault!"

There is a deep-lying sensitivity in A's that makes them want to look beneath the surface of things. If a husband is being constantly aggressive, for instance, the A wife's first reaction is not to say "He's like that," but to try to smooth it out.

It can take A's a while to identify a problem, but when they do they are quick to tackle it. Angela, an A nurse in her mid-forties, says:

> In the morning, breakfast is a special time for us because we both work, so we don't get to see each other till the evening. Marvin cooks bacon and eggs, and I get the newspaper and set the table with real care—it's a kind of ritual. But Marvin can be moody, sometimes even nasty. He'll attack me for stupid things like putting little bread plates out instead of taking the bread directly from the basket. Or he'll ask why I'm folding the napkins in such a ridiculous way. When he's like that, the message is loud and clear: "You're such an idiot, Angela, you make me sick!" This has been going on for years. I took it as a sort of morning mood until I realized there must be something behind it. Then I sat down and thought about it, and suddenly it struck me that sex was behind it. Marvin often wants to have sex before we get up, and I'm just not a morning person! I thought back, and sure enough, those mornings we did have sex, he was all sweetness and light. We talked about it, and funnily enough he wasn't even aware he was doing this. I saw his point, he saw mine, and we're dealing with it.

It is important in a marriage to find a way of communicating one's standpoint—to have self-clarifying dialogues. And it is important for there to be *reciprocity* of communication: both partners must do their part. The A believes strongly in this and tries to involve his or her partner in a dialogue that can even out the rough edges in a relationship. Although the A is not by nature as analytic as the B, A's do like to analyze their reactions and the reactions of their spouses, in the search for strategies to fend off future problems.

But once A's are on an analytic roll they can find it hard to stop. Things the spouse said years earlier can come back in haunting shapes and forms as the A dissects, weighs, and rationalizes why this or that was said or done. Toshitaka Nomi warns that A husbands can be particularly hard to live with: "Type A husbands are the most likely to drive their wives insane with petty badgering, nit-picking and other forms of nonviolent, and mostly unintended, torture."

When both partners are extreme A's, the process of conflict resolving can run itself into the mud. Seth, an A lawyer in his thirties, says that when he and his A wife start their "heavy-duty" talks the fur can fly:

> There are times when my wife and I start talking things through and we get deeper and deeper into why we did what, when, and how often. We wonder, "What triggered this, what triggered that?" "Was it anger at this, or anger at that?" "Were you acting hostile because . . . ?" and so on. Sometimes we get too deep into this, and then we scramble like hell to get out. It's like some kind of analytic swamp that we run aground in. It can get so bad that we finally burst out laughing at how funny we are. At such times it's humor and humor alone that saves our asses. I still think it's better, though, to talk about things, especially when you're really close with your wife. It's better this way than just pretending that a problem isn't there.

As Seth says, avoiding conflict altogether can be a dangerous tactic. A's are temperamentally introverted, and as a result can, in extreme cases, clam up after repeated failed attempts at tackling problems. The dangerous *ostrich syndrome*, where one or both partners close their eyes to marital trouble, can cause a pileup of unresolved issues, and ultimately send the marriage skidding. A's who fall into this trap run the risk of finding themselves in an empty relationship, in which the couple goes through the motions of having a warm and loving marriage, acting affectionately to each other, but harboring repressed anger and resentment.

A's are highly motivated for intimacy with people they love. In personality tests performed in the United States by the renowned psychologists Raymond Cattell, H. Bourtuline Young, and J. D. Hundleby, A's revealed themselves as "tender-minded" individuals, who are overprotective as well as sensitive.

A's are good by nature at dealing with private issues. They are reflective and inward-looking, in tune with what is happening inside their minds. But sometimes A's can get too caught up in introverted reflection to be aware of what their spouse is going through. Like B's, A's can become too self-involved and sometimes need a little prod to goad them out of their private world.

A's are hypersensitive and easily wounded. They often catch themselves watching their spouses' moves to see how the spouse feels toward them. Even in deeply intimate relationships A's can be vulnerable and insecure. As French specialists have stressed, the A is the most *harmonique* of the blood groups, and consequently will go to extremes to keep the status quo.

Harold, an A carpenter from New England in his early fifties who is married to an AB schoolteacher, says that rationality along with a dosage of tenderness has been a helpful ingredient in his marriage:

> My wife and I get along well. At least now we do. The kids are at school and we have more time for each other. In the past, we used to fight all the time, even during our honeymoon. We felt we weren't really compatible. I tried to make things right, but everything I'd do would make things worse. It was hard, we were thinking of divorce. But

we always loved each other, and we came to realize how important that is. Our fights now are really few and far between. If she seems upset about something I just ask her if she's OK, was it something I did? By now I can tell if something's bothering her, even if it's the slightest thing.

Marriage brings with it change, and this, interestingly enough, is one of the most difficult hurdles for the A to jump. As Harold says, the earliest part of his marriage was also the stormiest. The most difficult transition in a relationship for the A is the initial moving in together—in a traditional marriage, the period right after the wedding. Most couples, regardless of their blood types, are ill prepared for how problematic this period can be. But A's naturally shy away from change, and consequently are the hardest hit. After the never-never land of courtship, newlyweds move in together and have to immediately drop lifelong habits. Simple things like sleeping in the same bed, using the same bathroom, watching *Oprah*, not baseball, can have a rattling effect—especially for the A's who are so firmly set in their ways.

The A credo is that having deep feelings for a partner is not enough—what makes a good marriage is a rational approach to problems and a creative approach to surviving them. Ultimately the A's strongest point is that they try, each in his or her own way, to introduce thoughtfulness and good communication into their marriages and to develop joint activities with their spouses.

The Married B

Specialists have labeled B's as cool, distant, cerebral, driven. Hans Eysenck, a world authority on the psychology of personality, even calls them "neurotic."

Can B's, these extreme rationalists, score high on intimacy? Can you marry a B and keep the marriage happy?

Despite the low grades specialists have given B's on the emotional front, they have quite a few elements in their temperament that make them potentially the best spouses. In *Blood Groups and Personality*, the Japanese psychologist Y. Suzuki identifies optimism and decisiveness as two of the B's most prominent features. These qualities begin working powerfully in their favor from their first steps in a marriage. When B's love someone, they don't hesitate. They are quick to make up their minds, and they express their feelings loud and clear. This clarity in disclosing their attitudes communicates an unambiguous message of where the B stands, which makes it easier for the other partner to decide "Shall we go ahead?" In other words, when one of the two betrothed is a B, marriage arrangements are usually made quickly; when both are B's, the "I do!" can be almost instantaneous, circumstances permitting.

B's tend to be *rapid-involvement partners*: When they meet the right person, they know it, and if the response is equally strong on both sides then the B is prepared to commit to a relationship immediately.

Carol, a thirty-three-year-old B painter, married to Rod, a thirty-year-old B lawyer, says that despite their Catholic backgrounds their attraction for each other pushed them to "rapid involvement":

> I met my husband for the first time by the olives in our local supermarket. When I saw him I almost fell over. He was so beautiful, tall, and sensitive looking! I never thought this kind of thing could happen, especially not to me. I mean, not in a supermarket, anyway! . . . I'm Catholic, so I snatched up some olives and escaped to another aisle. And there he was again, like an apparition.

I couldn't get away! I kept staring at him and couldn't believe I was doing it. "Carol," I said to myself, "you're picking up men in the supermarket! Where is this going to lead?"... I paid, and he was at the next checkout counter. I left, and he followed. I hurried down the street, but not quite fast enough for him not to be able to catch up. Ten minutes later we were in my apartment. I couldn't believe it! It turns out, he couldn't believe it either, and he's Catholic, too! He was a lawyer and single. I had been reading some Pushkin short stories, and it turned out he had studied Russian as well as law, and he'd read Pushkin in the original. Well, that was the clincher! The rest is too X-rated to talk about, but four months later we got married.

Psychologists call couples who meet and marry fast "accelerated." In *Personal Relationships 2*, Huston, Surra, Fitzgerald, and Cate point out the surprising fact that "accelerated" courtship often results in better harmony in a marriage. Couples who are quick in their decision to marry seem to make the transition to married life more easily and effectively than couples whose courtship is long and drawn out.

Once married, the B's technical flair comes into its own. Social psychologists agree that a good marriage has to be worked at by both partners; it doesn't just happen. Love is not enough to ensure marital stability: The more mundane aspects of maintaining a marriage, like organizing finances, housekeeping, and the sharing of decision making, take center stage. Qualities such as steadfastness, perseverance, logic, and planning are vital—and B's score high on all of these.

B's tend to see their marriage as a project that needs constant work. Modern research has shown that couples who are the best organized are also the happiest. B's are pragmatic: If it makes sense, they are for it. So they tend to approach day-to-day married life with thoughtful organization.

The successful B maps out communicative strategies, aiming for a frank exchange of feelings and concerns. Household chores and child care are shared in a way agreeable to both partners. Leisure time is planned so that both husband and wife can relax together doing activities they both enjoy. Eric, a B editor and novelist, says:

> I'm very organized in my approach to marriage. My wife and I have been a solid team for over thirty years, and one of the many reasons is because we have worked out a logical system for dealing with the humdrum side of matrimony. We've both had full-time careers in publishing all along, so household chores, for instance, have always been equally shared. Things we enjoy doing, like cooking, we do together. Things we don't like doing, like dishes or bathrooms, we do on a rotating schedule. This way, neither of us gets saddled with all the dull chores.

The B's straightforward, logical approach does have its downside, however: B's can also be susceptible to the authoritarian side of their temperament. If they are convinced that they are right and their spouses are wrong, they are capable of bulldozing through issues, and laying down the law—their law.

The French psychologist Léone Bourdel says that this ordered approach is part of the B's *rythmique* quality. In *Blood Groups and Temperaments*, she writes about the B's self-assurance and superb talent for order, which, when it comes to their adaptability, have good and bad sides:

> Among all the blood groups, the B's way of adapting is the most rational, the most systematic, and the most methodical. The B incorporates all the elements of his own expe-

rience, reconciling everything to his own specific rhythm without the least concern for people's reactions. The B will even strive to impose his own rhythm on his environment, which he only becomes aware of whenever his surroundings clash with his rhythm.

The single most important element behind the B's approach to marriage is their deeply ingrained feeling that they bear responsibility for what happens to them—their *internal locus of control*. The B's temperament tells them that they alone are ultimately accountable for whether they feel happy with their marriages. When things go wrong, B's don't automatically throw up their hands and blame fate, or their spouses, lives, children, or jobs. "If something isn't working right," the B says, "then it's up to me to fix it."

The Married O

Nature has given the O all the tools for a successful and interesting marriage. O's are suave and extroverted, the most fun-loving among the blood types. They like going out, meeting people, and doing things that are unusual and challenging. When O's bring this lively sense of adventure to matrimony, sparks fly.

O's have a *prosocial* approach to marriage. They try to remain cheerful and warm in their relations with others, even when things get rough. They have a knack for humor, and there is an evenness, almost a fluency, in their interpersonal tactics. Being extroverted by nature, O's have a stronger affinity with what is happening around them, rather than with what is happening inside them. While B's, for instance, might be focused on private thoughts, or A's on private feelings, O's are more likely to center their concentration on their partners.

O's are doers. They enjoy sharing activities, a strong factor in promoting oneness in a family. While B's tend to do things with their spouses because it is practical, O's think of joint activities as fun. And when the joint activities are enjoyable, the feelings about a partner reflect it.

Doing things together as a team can have a powerful effect on cementing a relationship. Multifaceted interaction helps strengthen intimacy in a marriage. After all, partners who spend as little time as possible with each other inevitably grow apart. Simple things like jogging together, eating meals together, or even watching favorite TV programs in each other's company can bring two people close.

Raphael, an O literary agent who lives in New York, talks about how household chores can take on a special signifi-cance between a husband and wife:

> After a whirlwind day at the office—sometimes it's more like a typhoon or a hurricane—I'm glad to get home. Home for me is like a safe haven, although I have two kids, a two-year-old and a six-year-old, so you can imag-ine! As far as my kids are concerned, I'm a family man in the broadest sense of the word. But, spending time alone with my wife whenever we can is particularly valuable to me. We do things together, little things. I'll wash the dishes, she'll dry. We'll go to the supermarket and do some heavy-duty shopping. Little, boring, every-day chores like this take on a special meaning when your job and your kids are ready to eat you up whole. Obviously my wife and I often feel the strain, but we have fun, too. Once a week, or every two weeks, we'll get a baby-sitter and then go off to the theater or to a nice restaurant— champagne, caviar, dancing. Life's hard, but it should be fun, too!

The O's single strongest trait is their flexibility. After the wedding, when newlyweds have to come to grips with the nuts and bolts of married life, O's have the easiest time coping. They are not as susceptible to the intense stress that A's or B's feel when they are forced to change their set patterns of behavior.

This flexibility plays to the O's advantage throughout married life. O's generally don't fall into predictable patterns, which makes them more interesting as spouses. Like Raphael, they are spontaneous. They might decide they want to go to the theater ten minutes before curtain, or they might book a weekend cruise late Friday afternoon, sometimes overlooking mundane realities like whether they can afford it. Fun, for O's, is always more important than planned practicality. Matter-of-fact realism, the B's strong point, is a hard pill for O's to swallow, and their scintillating devil-may-care attitude can at times be a stumbling block.

In *Blood Groups and Temperaments*, Léone Bourdel calls the O *melodique*, a characterization inspired by the O's melodious suppleness:

> The O's adaptability is the most unconditional, the most complete of all the types. He lives his life like an evolving melody, constantly adapting himself to the different variations of his outer world, to events, to circumstances, to people and things. The O has a tendency to spontaneously integrate himself into his surroundings, to fully immerse himself, changing when the surroundings change, evolving with them—without being in the lead, but without dallying, either.

But too much adaptability in a marriage can have its problematic side. If there is inequity between a couple—when unresolved conflicts put a disproportionate amount of strain on one of the partners—there are two basic ways of dealing with it. You can face the problem head-on and try to resolve it, or you can adjust your psychological attitude—in other words, learn to live with the problem. O's often tend to do the latter.

Their natural flexibility can make them overadaptive, so instead of trying to resolve a conflict, they prefer to live with it, which can be difficult, even disastrous, in the long run.

It is important for O's that their partners understand their need for action and change. O's feel stifled by strict routine, and this can become a particular problem with sex. O's need surprises: sex at unusual times, in different positions, maybe even in different rooms. They also like as much variation as possible in the duration of sex: sometimes short and passionate, sometimes long and romantic—anything to break the routine. Sex on schedule is unsettling for the O.

In *You Are Your Blood Type*, Toshitaka Nomi warns that when pushed in the wrong direction, O husbands can become surprisingly dull. The bride who thought she had married a party animal now stands back in horror:

> Once he is married, an O man who was the life of the party as a single man can become sullen and ill-tempered. Whenever he is out in public, his former good cheer will suddenly resurface. This may seem stressful to a wife, but the only solution is to try to make life at home as peaceful as possible, avoiding the intrusions of the outside world. He was always like this when he was alone, but now he is doing it with a partner.

As Nomi points out, the O's skill at successfully relating to a group of people does not always translate to successful dyadic interaction—relating one-on-one. According to personality tests performed by the Chinese specialist K. H. Mee, O's scored high in emotional stability but low when it came to interpersonal relationships.

O's tend to be what social psychologists define as *independents* in their marriage style. Companionship and sharing are as important to them as having their own space, both physically and psychologically. O's are in many ways the most practical and enthusiastic of the blood groups. Once problems of routine and overadaptability have been dealt with, O partners can make the best spouses.

The Married AB

The AB's matrimonial strong point is their uncanny capacity to reinvent themselves. It is a form of temperamental pliancy that distinguishes them from the other blood groups. AB's are in tune with their spouses—they can pick up the subtlest signals of their partners' emotional states in an almost uncanny way, anticipating and fixing conflicts even before the first telltale signs appear. The AB's instinct and insight often make them the steadying cornerstone of the marriage, the emotional fixers when problems arise.

The Japanese psychologist Y. Suzuki stresses that empathy and altruism—their deep selflessness when their partners need help—are the AB's salient features. AB's can internalize what their partners express. They are good at assimilating things and providing support and comfort. Their strong desire to promote the welfare of their spouses on all levels is a powerful trigger of marital intimacy. This trait is the AB's special and individual form of *personalness*, which makes them stand apart as spouses.

European specialists have pointed out that the AB temperament is the most elaborate and complex of all the blood types. Chinese psychologist K. H. Mee actually gives AB's the highest marks for intuition, carefulness, and personal planning, but the lowest marks for emotional stability. The AB's many layers of sensitivity and feeling can make them volatile and full of surprises, but also gives them a deeper pool of emotional experience in relation to their spouse.

Marty, a B designer in his midthirties, is married to Michelle, an AB ballerina. He speaks of Michelle's "uncanny capacity" for emotional support:

> I would say Michelle can see right through me—in an emotional sort of way. I sometimes get overobsessive, I think. I grab hold of something—an idea, a problem— and I just can't let go. I design fashion jewelry, and before a big international show I have to come up with hundreds of new designs, so I can get quite demented. When I go off the deep end, Michelle has an uncanny capacity to sense how to handle me. Even when she is completely focused on her dancing or is in the middle of a ballet season, she'll always be there 100 percent for me. When I'm having an anxiety attack, her words and actions put things right.

AB's believe that constructive communication is important to the functioning of their relationships. Like the A's, AB's want things at home to run as harmoniously as possible. But unlike A's, AB's are what some social psychologists call *separates* in their marital outlook—although they want a close emotional bond with their partners, direct interdependence and physical togetherness are not as important to them. In other words, AB's want themselves and their partners to be able to develop and exercise their individuality. The AB believes that freedom and a certain amount of space can act to enhance the relationship, helping keep the marriage fresh. Partners who follow their own personal interests and pursuits have more perspectives that they can bring into the relationship than do partners who are too interdependent.

AB's seem to require a certain amount of "time-out" from their partners' company in order to feel a renewed energy for their relationships. This AB need for physical and psychological space is often one of the main causes of marital discord, as spouses misread the AB's quest for separateness as a sign of the AB's disinterest. The more AB's are pressured to neglect their pursuits outside the marriage, the more reticent they become, and if the issue is not confronted, communication can break down.

The biggest problem in this case is *polarization*, with the AB saying, "I need more freedom!" and the partner saying, "I need to be closer to you!" Over a period of time this can lead to *self-summarizing*, in which each partner takes an increasingly exaggerated view of his or her position and needs. Each partner begins overstressing a single element, sometimes of minor importance, identifying it as the crux of the problem:

"All you think about is your job!"
"You can't wait to get to that health club of yours!"
"Your damn car is more important to you than I am!"

The more the couple polarizes, the harder it is for them to tackle the more serious underlying problems that might be causing the friction—not seeing the forest for the trees.

Bill, an AB professor, says that he and his wife, Martha, a B professor, have disparate views of togetherness, which often cause them to clash:

I like getting out of the house. My wife, Martha, doesn't. It's an ongoing problem for us. Martha's a practical person who enjoys working at home, and she's chained to her computer. She belongs to a specialized talk group that spends hours and hours going over medieval Norse issues—that's her research specialty at the university. This might surprise you, but Norse studies is quite a cantankerous field, with professors getting into nasty arguments about what Knut the Green Dwarf really said, and whether it is to be taken as an allegorical reference to mushroom poisoning—things like that. . . . I, on the other hand, never touch the computer. I like meeting people you can shake hands with. I belong to the local choir, I'm one of the town supervisors, I'm on the Summer Arts Festival committee. . . .

I'm not saying my wife's the arguing type, but her take on things is that I'll do anything to get away, while she wants us to be together, to be close, to be one. But I point out to her that what it usually boils down to is that she wants me to be home, near her, quietly reading a book while she's fighting on the Internet. She laughs and sees my point; I see hers, too. Deep down I agree that I put a bit too much emphasis on activities away from home.

It is natural for couples to have different views of what closeness, sharing, and intimacy really are, and how much they need at any given time. As in Bill and Martha's case, open and frank discussions about what each partner perceives to be the source of the problem is important to avoid destructive pent-up resentments.

Toshitaka Nomi warns that AB husbands, in Japan at least, crave different forms of "social effectiveness" outside the home—sometimes to the point of neglecting their families:

When an AB husband starts spending time away from home, it is most often because he is with friends who share a hobby or some other interest with him. For a tiny minority of AB's, that hobby or interest is sex, and these become notorious Casanovas with multiple relationships constructed one upon another. . . . AB husbands are so obsessed with being socially effective do-gooders that they often leave the home fires unattended and consequently undernourished. Quite frankly, they easily neglect their responsibilities and have to be reminded of bills to pay, repairs to be made, and other routine matters.

AB's have a powerful imagination that they use often to try to flee from "routine matters." It is a form of emotional creativity that AB's use to help liven up a relationship. The AB's credo is that successfully mapping out all the day-to-day elements of living together needs more than just practicality—it needs originality, inventiveness, and surprise tactics.

CHAPTER VI

MARRIAGE COMPATIBILITY

A and A

Marriages where both partners are A's have an organized, low-key tone. But A's are also hypersensitive and easily hurt. Most clashes occur because one of the partners feels offended; then the veneer of calmness cracks, and disputes can be quite heated.

As French specialist Gille-Maisani warns, the A type "is generally an introvert, usually reserved, even inhibited, but *exuberant* when he explodes."

A's are creatures of habit. The A is happiest when the days, weeks, and months flow by smoothly: Scheduled amounts of time are set aside for work, leisure, chores, joint activities, and activities that the partners pursue alone.

Because both A partners like predictability, sex can become a clockwork ritual in which timing, position, and endurance are all preordained. But the A's don't mind! Actually, they enjoy the ritualized aspect of sex. Repetitiveness for the A is an important symbol of closeness. Doing the same things over and over with the person you love is comfortingly intimate. The only problem that might arise is if one of the partners isn't satisfied with some part of the ritual: One of them might want the experience to be romantically mellow, with much time spent on sensual foreplay, while the other might prefer short, powerful, passionate sex.

That's when the A's strong point—clear-cut communication—usually comes to the rescue. Both A partners try to talk their problems through and work hard at finding a solution—but not in bed.

According to Toshitaka Nomi, when A's are in bed words elude them: "They can share a strong sexual relationship without ever talking."

A and B

A's are organized in a creative way, B's in a technical way. As a couple, the A and B forge ahead in marriage as an effective, well-mobilized team, complementing each other's strengths.

Both A's and B's are particularly adept at handling the nuts and bolts of marriage maintenance—the A's with innovative idiosyncrasy, the B's with unremitting persistence.

The Japanese specialist Y. Suzuki considers optimism and decisiveness to be the B's top qualities, while patience and responsibility distinguish the A's. He adds that the A lacks the firmness and resolution of the B, while the B lacks the A's intuitiveness. On these points, the A and B partners definitely complement each other.

A's and B's are also compatible on the sex front. B's have a technical, no-nonsense approach to sex: They know what is effective, and doing well in bed to please their partners means a lot to them. A's, on the other hand, even though they enjoy routine, can be creative in subtle ways. As in the A-and-A partnership, once the management of sexual desires, patterns, and frequency is set the A and the B make a happy couple, although Toshitaka Nomi accuses them of spending more time "fantasizing about sex than actually doing it."

If sexual difficulties arise, relationship stress for the A and B can become particularly strong. But as both blood types tend to be clear-thinking, almost cerebral, in their approach to problems, solutions are usually reached quickly.

The problems of the A and B couple usually come from their both being assertive. A's can be gently manipulative, in a delicately nitpicking sort of way, while B's can sometimes bulldoze their way through difficult situations. But since both are reasonable, when a crisis develops, A and B partners are capable of stepping back and looking at the issues objectively.

A and O

A's and O's make good but uneasy partners. A's are basically introverted, O's extroverted. A's like predictability; O's want adventure. A's are usually understated and shrink from demonstrative verbal expression; O's are at ease passionately voicing their feelings. "The O places great importance on impulsive, free-flowing feeling, and a lesser importance on control by the will," writes the German psychologist Karl H. Göbber. "For the A, it is the exact opposite."

"Opposites attract," and this is precisely what makes the A-and-O marriage work. One partner's weaknesses are the other's strengths. Where A's lag, the O's pull them along.

A's find O's exciting and interesting. They admire their

free, outgoing nature, while O's find the A's depth and aplomb intriguing.

The major hurdle in an A-and-O marriage is the partners' incompatible views on routine. A's find routine pleasant, while O's find it oppressive. O's want to go out more with their spouses, throw parties, meet people—the A's don't. For the A, romantic evenings at home, even spent sitting together in front of the TV, are so much nicer.

The most important issue for O's and A's early in their relationships is sex: how, when, and how often. The A is happy with a same-place-same-time system, while the O prefers different positions, durations, and intensities.

Once A's and O's come to terms with the fact that they have opposing temperaments, and that this is what attracted them to each other in the first place, they make the most successful couple.

A and AB

In many ways A's and AB's are alike: Both have strong creative streaks, both are temperamental—AB's more so than A's—and both are prepared to work hard at supporting the other emotionally.

Many scientists have compared the qualities of these blood groups. Research by the Swiss specialist Maurer-Groeli indicates that A's are more apt to own up to their errors than are AB's. Suzuki says that A's and AB's each have a strong capacity for altruism—empathy and selflessness—when it comes to dealing with their partners' feelings. K. H. Mee adds that both blood types tested high on "carefulness," although the AB, according to his research, is more resolute when it comes to making decisions than the A.

In a marriage, the A acts as a strong anchor for the AB's

sometimes volatile nature. AB's find it hard to control their temperament, which makes them naturally more creative than the other blood groups, but also potentially more explosive. The Indian specialist V. V. Jogawar points out that A's are by nature placid and self-sufficient. A's are also prepared, when necessary, to take the extra conciliatory step toward settling an argument with their spouses.

With the AB there is never a dull moment, and after years of living with them, partners are still surprised by things they do or say. For the A, the element of surprise in the AB is attractive, but also unnerving. A's feel uncertain when they can't predict their partners' moves.

So in A-and-AB marriages, A partners often find themselves periodically feeling slightly restless in the relationship.

Sexually, A's and AB's are extremely compatible. The AB has a fluid, almost unstructured approach and yet doesn't mind the A's penchant for routine, which the AB actually finds enjoyable. AB's, with the most complex temperament of all the blood types, enjoy structure but find it hard to impose it themselves. With A's there to do it for them, AB's feel secure and organized.

B and B

In the B-and-B marriage, each partner manages to maintain a surprising amount of space and privacy. Experts worldwide agree that B's are generally independent of their environment and have a powerfully developed sense of self. B's place great importance on pursuing their interests, and by extension they support their spouses' need for independence.

The B-and-B marriage is often the most productive kind, with each partner inspiring the other to self-development.

They usually find the other B to be the perfect spouse—it is easier to relate to someone if they are exactly like you.

But when the B's competitive drive becomes overdominant, destructive conflict can arise. When one B thinks that what he or she is doing is more important than what the partner is doing, problems inevitably occur. In this case, B's can become overbearing and try to impose their own goals on their spouses. Both B partners have an innate tendency to be stubborn and tenacious. For B's, the danger lies in slipping into what is known as a *half-shell marriage*, in which the partners might be fond of each other, even happy together, but find it hard to live together.

The B's strongest characteristics are clarity and directness. When there's a problem, B's usually manage to address and solve it swiftly. The B-and-B couple is also proficient when it comes to sex. Married B's find it easier than most other types to discuss particulars—who enjoys what, when, and how often—in an objective, rational way. Toshitaka Nomi, however, disagrees: "Their performance and satisfaction are average. They don't get too interested in sex." This could be said of the B partners who pour all their energy into developing their careers.

B and O

In the 1930s, the blood-group pioneer Takeji Furukawa identified both the B type and the O type as being active. In marriage the two blood groups complement each other: B's are active in an organized, cerebral way, and O's in an organized but easygoing way.

Although B's and O's are alike in energy, they are almost exact opposites in temperament. The B is introverted, the O extroverted. B's like doing things on their own; O's like doing things with others. O's enjoy meeting people, going to parties, having a lot of commotion around them. B's don't.

Different though these two blood types are, they complement each other well in matrimony. As so often happens when opposites meet, they work smoothly together. The B appreciates the O's free, outgoing nature, while the O admires the B's infallible sense of direction. When the two join forces, the marriage can be extremely successful.

The first few months of matrimony are the hardest, as both partners struggle to establish as much common ground as possible. In this initial period the O proves the more flexible and the B the more systematic in dealing with day-to-day details. Once the initial rocky period is over, the B-and-O marriage usually works well.

B's and O's have very different approaches to sex. In bed B's are truly *rythmique*, they prefer an ordered, systematic approach. Expertise, not variety, is the B's strength. O's, on the other hand, are typically *mélodique* in bed—they like as much diversity and variation as possible. The B's adroitness and the O's flexibility usually work well together. As Toshitaka Nomi says, "They like to teach each other new, ever more exciting techniques."

B's and O's both have great interpersonal skills: The B is good at relating one-on-one in a calm, reflective way, while the O is more open and generally expansive. In a B-and-O marriage, these different attitudes give a sharp punch to the partners' interaction.

B and AB

The AB qualities that a B finds most attractive are flexibility and originality. The B qualities that an AB finds most attractive are the strict sense of order and perseverance in whatever the B does.

Both blood types admire the characteristics in the other that they themselves lack. When AB's marry B's, their combined talents make them a powerful team. AB's use their many interests to reach their goal, while B's follow through on what they do with single-minded conviction.

Many specialists have made psychological comparisons of these two blood types. V. V. Jogawar found that AB's are generally less tense than B's; David Lester and Jeri-Lynn Gatto have determined that AB's are more extroverted than B's; Dr. K. H. Göbber put forward the notion that "as a compound group, AB's can, depending on the circumstances, lean toward A's or even B's in temperament."

However strong their character differences are, both blood types work hard at initiating and maintaining self-clarifying dialogue right from the start of a marriage. B's, with their deep subjectivity and independence from their environment, sometimes take blinkered, even dogmatic, positions, while the AB is extraordinarily flexible. When the B's dogmatic attitude takes over, the AB is the only blood type able to counter it.

The AB's sex drive is generally stronger than the B's, and their approach to sex is definitely more *"complexe."* AB's want sex to have an element of unpredictability and suddenness, while B's prefer to plan ahead. But AB's are the most adaptable of the blood types. Even if they and their B spouses find their sexual rhythms unsynchronized, AB's gladly compromise.

Despite their differences, B's and AB's are remarkably alike, making space for themselves as individuals within their marriages. In this sense, the B-and-AB marriage is extremely compatible. Each partner understands and appreciates the other's strong sense of self.

O and O

The O couple is flexible, adventurous, and outgoing. Both partners enjoy socializing, meeting new people, and having fun. When O's team up together, life can be extremely upbeat.

O marriages usually fall into two distinct categories. In the first, the O partners form a strong duo in which they do things together, nurture the same interests, mix with the same people, and try to have as much fun as possible *together*. In the second, the O partners are just as outgoing and enterprising, but the husband has his life, his hobbies, and his friends, and the wife hers.

Both types of O couples are happy with the way their marriages are organized, since O's basic need is the freedom to get out and do things.

O's are extroverts with a sharp sense of the world around them and what is happening in it. Consequently, they relate to their partners in an external, objective way. When issues come up, O's are immediately aware of them. Gille-Maisani points out that the O "pays great attention to circumstances; he seeks to resolve problems by conciliation."

O's are particularly well suited to each other sexually. Both are adventurous and adaptable in bed. Of all the blood groups O's have the least guilt, anxiety, and shyness when it comes to sex. Hans Eysenck, a world-renowned authority in the psychology of personality, writes in *Sex and Personality* that according to his tests, people who score high in extroversion tend to have more sex.

But the O's supple and adaptable nature also has its downside. When the marriage goes through turbulent periods, the O's can be too quick to adapt to the adverse situation instead of addressing the problems. In cases of constant adjustment without resolution, they might find themselves in an *empty shell marriage*, in which the pair stays together despite the fact that they are not satisfied.

O and AB

Specialists have classed the O and AB as the two most extroverted blood types. They are both naturally outgoing, and are compatible in their dynamic and venturesome approach to marriage. What makes the O-and-AB match particularly interesting is that while both are open and gregarious, O's have a relaxed relationship with others, while AB's are much more intense. Even though O's are energetic and always ready for fresh projects, they do not have the AB's almost obsessive need to see things through, to get things perfect. This casual quality in O's often gives them the reputation of being enthusiastic but impractical—of setting unrealistic goals for themselves.

In an O-and-AB marriage, the AB is often the partner who introduces an important element of practicality and eye for detail that an O-and-O marriage might lack. The O-and-AB match is positive and productive. Both types are doers and both are flexible, which can make the couple particularly successful in both day-to-day matters and in long-term projects that they undertake together. But there is one major potential area of conflict in O-and-AB marriages: the AB's requirement for space. As a matter of temperament AB's feel they have to collect and organize their thoughts without interruption. The expansive O does not always understand this need for privacy, and as a result arguments often result.

The O-and-AB couple is sexually compatible: Both are extroverts, which, according to Hans Eysenck, indicates both a heightened interest in sex and less guilt about it. For the O-and-AB marriage, sexual adjustment and marital adjustment to a large extent go hand in hand. Because both O's and AB's are interested in adventure and variety, they are more open to communicating with each other on sexual matters and trying new positions and ideas.

AB and AB

The AB-and-AB marriage is the most energetic and tempestuous of all. When the two *complexe* temperaments meet, sparks fly.

AB's have colorful and rich inner lives. Most specialists have classed them as a "mixed group"; their temperament is made up of a jumble of the qualities typical of the other blood types. The general consensus is that you never know what the AB will do next.

It is the element of volatility that makes the AB-and-AB marriage so interesting. AB partners maneuver the elements of their relationships almost like a pleasurable but high-powered chess game. Each move is a surprise to the other. While AB's who are in relationships with A's or B's might go to great lengths to adapt their mercurial complexity to these more stable blood types, when two AB's marry, their intricate inner lives can flourish unhampered.

This union has its positive and negative sides. The positive side is that the AB has the temperamental resources and talents to go further and reach goals faster than other blood types, and when two AB's join forces they can energize and inspire each other. The negative side is that AB's have a difficult time keeping themselves in check. In this sense, two AB's together can create high tension that results in clashes.

When AB partners are in tune with each other their sexual

relation is involved and complex. Because this couple is the most extreme in its harmony or discord, sex can be frequent and passionate, or rare and frosty. Toshitaka Nomi puts it in a nutshell: "The possibilities are endless. These two can both be extremely harmonious in sex or totally miserable."

The basic truth about the AB-and-AB couple is that they are not into stability. On all levels, their relationship is either energetic and creative, or quarrelsome and rough.

CHAPTER VII

BLOOD TYPES AND MONEY

A's and Money

A's are organized, in charge, patient, able, *harmonique*—and yet money can ruffle even the calmest A.

A's fall into two clear-cut money groups: In one group are the *entrepreneurial* A's, who plot and strategize, who enjoy the technicalities of carefully nurturing their assets. They are the most circumspect denizens of the money-making world. They gravitate to minimum-risk speculation—government bonds, T-bills, CDs—but their watchful approach usually pays off. In the second group are the *hands-off* A's, who are financially inhibited, anxious about money, and have an almost phobic approach to their personal finances. These A's have a deep-rooted sense that dealing with money drains energy that they should be investing elsewhere. They find thinking about money tiring, even boring.

Rich or poor, A's are temperamentally insecure when it comes to money. They weigh and counterweigh every financial move. This reticence explains why most A investors prefer mutual funds over individual stocks. Entrepreneurial A's are good at building a successful business, as there is a structure to the process, a blueprint to follow, but they stall out when it comes to making the simplest investment decisions. A's feel safer leaving all the moves to a tried and trusted institution with a staff of security analysts who have defined, clear-cut investment strategies. A's take the term "security" seriously.

Frank, an A investor in his early fifties who lives in New York, says that he likes to do all his own market analysis so that he stays in charge of his own money. But he stresses the importance of having a broker who is with a reliable firm to help him make the crucial decisions:

> I enjoy the challenge of investing and I've made a lot of money. When I say "I," I mean that my broker has consistently placed my money well, overall. It took me a long time to settle on someone I trust, but I looked hard, did my research, and found a broker I've stayed with. . . . Securities have always fascinated me, but you need a good adviser. I love doing the technical things, like studying the markets, seeing what the sectors and companies are doing, looking for the perfect underpriced asset. But making a move to buy this security or sell that one always makes me break out in a sweat. I don't want to make mistakes or take stupid risks just because I don't have the information that a brokerage firm has. I mean, those guys work ten-hour days. . . . The variables in the market are infinite, and there's no way a guy like me can make a real decision. I do my homework, I always know what's going on—but let the real experts come up with the goods.

A's respect the technicians—the "real experts," as Frank calls them—who have a more detailed understanding of a field than they do. When they are investing, A's mix their innate insecurity with practicality. They like to do the ground-work, but not to make the decisions.

There is, however, a mild opportunistic streak in A investors that manages to break through their natural self-restraint. A's who are interested in the highest safe yield for their money do best in limited partnerships. Here A's can still exercise their analytical and creative skills in an area of risk that can provide higher returns. Ultimately, regardless of whether or not A's relegate their financial dealings to a broker, they still like the feeling of having accomplished something when an investment brings a good return. Seth, an A lawyer who sees investing as a "second career," says:

> I like hitting the jackpot. It's the greatest feeling when an investment pans out. But whether I'm working with a broker or not, I like the kind of investment where I can say that I did the research and then the money rolled in. For me, finding a winner by accident is no fun. It's not the money, it's the feeling that I made things happen that is the most important element in my investments.

A's, rich or poor, have much more of an emotional rela-tionship to money than do other blood types. Under stress, A's often find themselves turning to money as a mechanism to reduce anxiety. The A feels:

> "I'm having a bad day, I'm going shopping!"
> "I hate my job, I'm going shopping!"
> "My relationship's a mess, I'm going shopping!"

Stress spending can range from a trip to the supermarket to manic shopping at a mall. The stressed-out A finds working off tension with a credit card particularly rewarding, since the card, symbolically at least, represents a limitless flow of cash. The freedom of unbounded spending is more intoxicating than shopping with one or two fifty-dollar bills.

Jake, a New York–based A journalist, talks about trips to his local bookstore just before stressful deadlines:

> I've been a journalist for years, but I've only just realized that when the pressure is on I work off my nervousness by shopping. I buy books, nothing else. And not a lot, just ten here, ten there—the kind of books I wish I had, but which I would never buy in the cold light of day. When I'm on one of these binges I feel, "I'm having a hard time, New York's getting to me, I can't stand the stress my editor is putting me under! What the hell, I deserve these books!" . . . I don't see my book buying as a real problem, because I'm not bankrupting myself or anything. But I guess it's an interesting insight to how my brain works.

The unfortunate hitch in stress spending is that it offers only a short-term escape. After the initial exhilaration of book buying simmers down, Jake will take his books home, arrange them on the shelf, and dream about which one he will read first. But the initial stress triggers—the deadline, life in New York, problems with his editor—are still there and still unresolved.

In Jake's case, his emotional spending is harmless. His library might periodically grow by twenty or thirty volumes, but he is not jeopardizing his finances. Some A's find that they are capable of spending much larger amounts of money before their natural cautiousness cuts in. For these A's, the psychological aftermath is particularly tough to deal with. Jolted by the momentary loss of control, they panic, cutting back in a fit of *compulsive nonspending*. It's a dangerous cycle of anxiety, shopping, followed by even more anxiety, followed by more shopping.

Ideally, A's should rely on the levelheadedness and the reserved calm that characterize their blood type. Like B's, A's are attracted to system and order, which can ultimately work in their favor. It is important for all A's to face their finances head on, because an entrepreneurial spirit rests below the surface in every A.

The best advice for A's (and everyone) is to spend at least two hours a week organizing their money and mapping out an investment plan. They should take the time to study and understand how the financial and economic systems work.

Even for the hands-off A's, who are frightened of dealing with money, the world of securities and investment need not be dark and mysterious.

B's and Money

B's have a practical, no-nonsense approach to money: When it comes to finances, there is no positive or negative emotional response. For B's, cash is a means to an end, a stepping-stone that helps them get what they want. B's who are attracted to money are specifically attracted to the power it brings with it, because that power is measurable, countable down to the last cent. You can figure out what you are worth and calculate the assets available to you. This judicious element makes many B's economical spenders, bargain-minded to the extreme, who put an unusual amount of effort into finding the best goods at the best prices. B's can be remarkable dollar stretchers—some B's will drive fifteen miles to a supermarket featuring a sale instead of shopping at the neighborhood grocery and paying regular prices.

This penchant for saving is not a result of money anxiety;

B's are not scrimpers by nature. Their financial carefulness, whether mild or fanatical, is an exercise in rationality, a commonsensical approach to things and what they are worth. The B's point of view is that if you can get two for the price of one—and you need two—then it's illogical to pass up the offer.

In *Tempéraments psychobiologiques*, Gille-Maisani pointedly portrays the B as a type who strictly follows a private game plan. In finances, as in many other sectors, the B has no time for sentiment or decisions based on emotion. "The B's judgment is objective, critical; he despises sensitivity. He dreads anything that impedes his action. He is usually more convinced of determinism than he is of the importance of fulfilling responsibility."

The B's strong pragmatism comes to the fore in their investment patterns. B's like tangible, palpable investments; for instance, real estate is particularly attractive. You can *see* a piece of property that you have bought; you can add things to it, embellish it, put your own stamp on it. Even if a property loses value, it is still there. Andrew, a B investor from New York, says:

> I avoid stocks. I always have. They rise, they fall, they rise again. One minute they are worth this, the next minute that. I don't like that; I like to know where I am with my money, I like to be in control. It's as simple as that. With a stock you press three keys on your computer, and the money's out like a flash. I've made a lot of money—I know what I'm doing. I invest in things like coins, collectibles. You'd be surprised at the amount of money you can make with those things! If I really want to gamble, I dabble in real estate. It's more fun. Before I decide to buy, I look at the property, I look at the neighborhood, I look at all the records, everything. I bought into midtown

Manhattan just before they started cleaning up Times Square. It was so obvious the prices would skyrocket. Wherever I put my money, the bottom line is I want to call the shots!

The B wants to control things. Unlike A's, for instance, B's feel uneasy about ceding the management of their money to a broker or financial adviser. The B investors' confidence in money matters comes from their systematic and responsible approach to finance. B's like to follow their own path, independent of their environment. B's who do invest through stockbrokers are the type of client who is constantly calling for advice but never takes it—unless the advice happens to coincide with what the B intended to do all along. As far as the B is concerned, money is a matter of personal responsibility.

B's who speculate prefer to own stocks directly. The B feels that there is more of a personal challenge involved in selecting stocks for themselves as opposed to mutual funds that rely on professional management.

B investors are good technicians and analysts, but they often falter when a sudden reversal requires flexibility. As Léone Bourdel writes in *Blood Groups and Temperaments*:

> The B functions according to his constant, on a personal rhythm. He is only able to respond to whatever he himself has conceived, decided, understood, or accepted, either spontaneously or as a result of rational deliberation.
> The true B does not adapt himself to his outside world, he does not try to interact harmoniously with it: he follows his path single-mindedly.

The B's rigid rhythm, which works well when it comes to the organization and administration of funds, can be problematic when quick decisions about market strategy need to be made. Most B's are aware of this weakness and stay away from high-risk investment. Marty, a B accessory designer from New York, talks about his experience in the stock market. Marty complains that he had problems "synchronizing" his money successfully with the market's fluctuations:

> I'm what you'd call a weekend investor: Investing supplements my income, but I make my living designing fashion accessories. I did very well with real estate during the mideighties and have been moving steadily ahead ever since. In the early nineties, for about a year or so, I was conned into buying stocks. Things were working out fine with my other investments, so I thought I might as well get into some higher-risk investing. I did it in an unusual way, through a "cold call"—some hard-selling woman from a brokerage firm called me on the phone, just like that, and said, "You're successful—let's work together, we'll double your money, we'll triple it!" I'm not the impulsive type, and I don't usually fall for that kind of line, but I went for it anyway. The stuff she sent me in the mail was impressive. It worked out well in the beginning—it was great—but in the long run it got too fast-paced for me. I couldn't synchronize myself with what the market was doing. I kept getting migraines. I made some money, but eventually I lost about ten thousand! So that's that. No more stocks for me!

Although B investors can be rigid in their reactions and consequently lose out on fast-paced ventures, they always take charge of their financial actions. It's their money they are investing, and their money is their responsibility. Marty is a typical B realist. He tried his hand at the stock market, and when he realized his temperament was getting in the way of success he pulled out and returned to the type of investment he felt more comfortable with.

The positive side of Marty as an investor is his *external locus of control.* He has a clear, rational view of what he is doing, and does not lose time and energy blaming the broker, the market, or the government for his losses.

The best financial advice for B's is to take a step back and rationally weigh their strengths and weaknesses. B's are good at strategy, at clear organization of funds, and that is where their emphasis should be. B's are naturally self-reliant, independent, and action oriented—perfect qualities for money-making. B investors, like all investors, should put their assets in areas where they feel the most comfortable—regardless of whether that's coins, real estate, or rare Barbie dolls.

O's and Money

The O is the most materialistic of the blood types: Money brings excitement, power, action, freedom—and, most important, tangible things, things that can be bought.

The O's practical side urges them to plan ahead, to budget their incomes for short- and long-term goals, to organize their finances. But against this is their strong conviction that money is there to be made and spent. O's don't like to prepare themselves for a rainy day that might or might not come. Gille-Maisani points out that living in the moment is too important for the O: "Being more adaptable than the other temperaments, he is less provident: he is the type who grabs at the moment and at circumstances."

O investors enjoy moneymaking from a social perspective. They see money as power, but not as a stepping-stone to reaching personal goals, as B's do. The O sees money as a catalyst that sparks interaction with others. It helps them network, move up the ladder, get things done. For the quintessential O, making money is a group activity. While A's and B's are generally lone entrepreneurial types, O's like the action of a crowd. They like pitching themselves against opponents, thus proving their cleverness. While A investors spend most of their energy plotting, and B investors organizing, O investors enjoy the actual transaction of moneymaking—the challenge of buying, selling, making deals, finding winners.

The O investor sees the securities market as a high-stakes game board. Before O's make their move they feel a surge of what psychologists call *pre-emotion*—the tingling rush of anticipation seconds before placing assets on potential winners. Graham, a New York investor and a typically unreserved O, says that he prefers being financially insecure to being bored. He prefers what he calls "a chance at striking gold" to having all his money tied up in minimal-risk investments:

Ninety percent of the fun in the investment game is the challenge. I don't like the safe and boring securities, but I'm a realist, so I keep some of my money—the absolute minimum—in surefire places, and then use the rest to play in quick-action areas. I get a real kick out of moving it around. You have to be on your guard, you have to be quicker than the next guy to see a winner. It keeps the adrenaline flowing—that's why I'm in this game. Other guys have a "candy-store" problem—everything looks good to them and they can't decide which is the best buy—not me! I have a sixth sense. When I get my hands on an underpriced security, it's a great feeling, even if I don't sell it for years. When I cash in a high stock at the right moment, it's like I'm at a winning table in Atlantic City.

The extroverted O likes competition and the action of making money in a group, and is also strongly motivated by the group's approbation when a winning number comes in. O's are particularly sensitive to their environment, and are galvanized by the applause, approval, and even the envy of their peers. But what makes O's best in the high-risk investment world is their quick flexibility at monitoring the pulse of the market. The Japanese specialist Y. Suzuki found that O's in all walks of life prefer challenging assignments and are not afraid of failure. As in Graham's case, O's actually prefer surprises to predictability. In moneymaking, they do best when a touch of jeopardy makes a transaction more interesting. The extroverted O has an almost hawkeyed sense of detail and is quick to notice changes. Léone Bourdel writes in *Blood Groups and Temperaments* that this is a natural expression of the O's *mélodique* nature:

> The O's response is always trained in the direction of a stimulus, taking into simultaneous consideration all the different elements of what is happening around him, proportionally to the elements' intensity. The O is the strongest of all the groups in this form of adaptability, as he has the ability to be both highly sensitive to his surroundings and at the same time move towards his goals swiftly and easily, using whatever possibilities are offered.

This "high sensitivity to his surroundings" gives the O what could be called a *predator* mentality—in the positive sense of the word. The O sees an opportunity and pounces before the A or B has had time to react. This readiness makes O's particularly good freelancers. A's and B's are happier with regular, fixed incomes, while the O is naturally more attracted to the idea of grabbing opportunities as they come. While other blood types might panic when their income fluctuates, O's are good at making realistic adjustments.

But for many O's, financial success is strongly tied to self-esteem. When money rolls in, self-evaluation is high—when money rolls out, it is low. O's have a special emotional bond to money. When they believe they are handling their finances right, they feel secure, enlivened, and ready to take on new projects. When they feel they are not handling their money well they can slip into a depression that specialists have dubbed *money sickness*. The O's feel despondent, out of control, and their self-esteem can plummet. Mark, a concierge in a New York hotel, says that a year ago his simple decision to aggressively take charge of his finances drastically swept away all symptoms of *money sickness*:

In the last twelve months I have finally taken charge of my finances. They were a mess—my credit card debts were half my salary, my student loans weren't getting paid off, checks were bouncing. Whenever I had to pay bills I felt I was entering a war zone, and my stomach would literally start churning. I'd draw from one credit card and pay the minimum on another. I'd "forget" to sign a check, I'd send the cable payment to my landlord "by mistake" just to get an extra few days' grace period on the rent. Sometimes I'd have to lie down after a morning spent paying bills. I felt like I'd overdosed on money shuffling. One day I simply said, "OK, that's enough," and got my finances organized: food money, rent money, bill money, pocket money—even money to be saved. I decided to focus on living as well as possible—that was really important to me—you know, going out, having fun, meeting people, and all that. But I also set strict financial goals and I stuck to them. Now I'm buying an apartment, and I've even invested in a growing firm in Pennsylvania. It's such a great feeling to make your money work!

Whatever their financial situation, O's are the most practical blood type in the sense that they are the most pliable. O's whose finances are in disarray find that it is not anxiety about money that keeps them back, but often simply a lack of motivation to get organized. The O's overflexible character often leads to complacency. It sometimes takes a simple but firm decision for the O to change long-standing habits. As in Mark's case, living well in the present is very important for all O's, and they manage better than other blood types to maintain the highest living standard their income allows, while still saving and investing.

The O's positive attitude is their strongest ally in money-making. The best advice for O's is to keep their strong points from becoming their weaknesses. In other words, to avoid being overoptimistic and overconfident—a light dose of caution is sometimes advisable. If O's are going to gamble in securities, they shouldn't always give in to the tingling feeling that one particular asset is a sure winner. Sometimes it is wise for the O's to bridle their enthusiasm.

O investors who enjoy gambling in high-risk securities should still take basic measures to protect their finances and avoid putting all their eggs in one basket.

AB's and Money

When it comes to money, the AB is the most impulsive and creative of all the blood types. You can't pin AB's down. Within seconds they can swing from financial optimism to anxiety: free-spending one moment, anxiously scrimping the next, strategically moving their assets with mathematical precision, then buying and selling recklessly. The French psychologist, Léone Bourdel poetically defines the AB as "the person of limitless possibility, the angel, the demon—the adolescent."

AB investors who have made it big have done so by being the most creative speculators on the market. AB's are the most sensitive of the blood types when it comes to tuning in to their environment. They have a flair for putting out feelers to probe for any information that might be useful to them. This is especially true for the AB investor, who has a lightning-quick eye for spotting fluctuations in the securities market that can increase the yield. Expert AB investors owe their successful strategizing to their sensitivity to details.

The AB investor approaches securities with the precision of a mathematician. This is a form of compensation, because AB's feel that their internal disorganization—the "adolescent" in them—needs to be held in check if they are going to get anything done.

John, an AB professor of comparative literature, has amassed a large fortune in stocks. "Two souls, alas! dwell in my breast," he says with humor, quoting the German literary giant Goethe, and defines his orderliness in financial matters as "setting up a floodgate to stop the onrush of disorganization":

> I am very pleased with the way my investments have been growing—I use a good and reliable broker in Boston. However, I'm not your average investor type who lives with his eyes glued to the exchange. Added to that, I'm extremely disorganized by nature. So how does one give lectures, direct doctoral dissertations, go to conventions, publish books and articles, and still have time to make money in securities? By being *extremely* organized! I read the *Wall Street Journal* and the *New York Times* before breakfast every day and see what the trends are. If there are any decisions to be made, I call my broker right away. I also always make a point of following up and investigating his

suggestions. If I didn't force myself to stay on top of my investments I'd be in trouble.

The Chinese specialist K. H. Mee found that AB's had the highest test scores for personal planning, intuition, and carefulness, and that they scored lowest on emotional stability. According to Suzuki, AB's have a strong dosage of hot temper and impatience. This mix of elements plays a vital role in the AB's approach to finances. As in John's case, most AB's find that if they don't keep their guard up, their financial decisions are all too often based on whatever mood they happen to be in.

In money matters the AB's are the most skeptical of the blood types. Their optimism can quickly swing toward pessimism, and AB's who aren't careful will let these swings affect their financial moves. When in an overly optimistic mood, AB's tend to indulge in impulsive speculations; when overly pessimistic, they can stagnate.

In the AB's view, doing well financially depends more often than not on luck and on being in the right place at the right time—hard work and dedication play only a minimal role. Because the AB temperament leans toward volatility, money symbolizes security and control. After a financial loss AB's, like A's, can fall into a period of *compulsive nonspending*, in which insecurity and anxiety keep all spending at a minimum. Even if the AB is financially secure, a deal gone wrong or a stock hitting an air pocket can turn into a symbol of impending disaster.

Anna, a New York AB photographer, talks about her husband's maniacal "budget cuts" when his investments go wrong:

> On October 19, 1987—Black Monday, when Wall Street crashed—my husband came home from the office, and I

knew immediately that disaster had struck. He was in the dumps for a whole year. It wasn't so much that he'd lost hundreds of thousands—it was the realization that he *could* lose hundreds of thousands that made him go off the deep end. That evening on Black Monday our budget at home was slashed! Richard started checking the food I bought, canceling plans for sending our son to private preschool—and forget the vacation! The silly thing was that we had more than enough money, and within seven or eight months he made back everything he'd lost. It was all in his mind. After Black Monday I decided that I would get my own career as a photographer back on track the minute my son was in preschool. That way I would be financially independent the next time there was a crash.

It is important for AB's to always work hard at keeping a realistic outlook about their money. When there is a financial reversal it is healthy to adapt one's spending and one's investment strategies, but it is important to do this rationally. Like Richard, most AB's tend to fall victim to the "halo effect": If something unfortunate happens to their finances, they see everything else in the light of that one incident.

The AB's mixed temperament is at its most pronounced in handling money. They have both the impulsiveness and the control of the typical A, the rationality of the B, and the interest in high-risk speculation of the O. The most successful AB investors are those who can coordinate and synchronize these incompatible drives within themselves. As K. H. Mee points out, there is an element of "cold-mindedness" in the AB—an orientation toward thinking instead of feeling. But when AB's become too adventurous in their financial speculating, this streak of cold-mindedness might well save the day.

The AB's *complexe* nature is both their strength and their weakness in financial matters. The best advice for AB's is to organize themselves and to keep their emotions out of their financial judgments. They should subdue the urge to make impetuous financial decisions without extensive analysis and assume full control over and responsibility for their money. As a result, confidence will replace anxiety.

The AB's natural aptitude to be the most creative investors plays in their favor. They have particularly keen perceptual skills. When pushed, AB's are capable of taking quick action and approaching financial problems with great versatility.

AB's who can combine their natural creativity with an organized and systematic approach to finances are bound to do well.

CHAPTER VIII

BLOOD TYPES AT PLAY

A's at Play

For A's, play is an escape from the constraints of work and everyday life. Leisure activities, such as hobbies and sports, bring freedom from role expectations and stress, freedom from things that *have* to be done. This is especially important for the introverted A who, more than other blood types, needs to unwind after interacting with people for long periods.

A's need what sociologists calls *nonobligated time,* time to themselves in which they can choose what to do and when to do it. Even if they have a demanding hobby with strict rules—like kayaking, rock climbing, or ballet—the fact that they have chosen this hobby and that it is not something that has been imposed on them is important. A's might have to go to work, but they don't have to play.

A's prefer two types of leisure: solitary leisure and time spent with one or two people they are close to. Most of the recreational activities A's enjoy can be done alone or in a small group: watching television, reading, jogging, going for walks. Even when A's are relaxing with friends or family they can still immerse themselves in what they are doing. A's can watch TV in a group but still be deeply immersed in it, just as they can spend an evening with their family while reading a book. This form of leisure is important to A's because it reinforces social solidarity with the people closest to them, but still allows them to focus on things that they themselves are interested in.

Jake, an A journalist, says that he watches a foreign-language film on video after work. It's a hobby that helps him unwind, but also an educational challenge. Jake might watch the film alone or with a friend, but either way it has become an important ritual:

> After a long day in interviews, chasing stories, relentless foot-slogging, I feel I need to chill out and tank up on energy. Whenever I have the chance after work, I pick up a foreign-language movie from a video club in Soho. Right now I'm in an Italian phase—Rossellini, Pasolini—I'm watching all the classics I can get my hands on. It's a hobby; I really enjoy it, but I also like the fact that I'm doing something for my "education." These movies help me work on my languages, but they're also an escape to different times and places. I've been doing this for at least two years now, and even though I do it for fun, I've become quite a specialist: I even did an article about film noir for a British magazine. So I guess it's no longer just a hobby. . . . Anyway, after a long day I need this time to myself, even if I'm watching a film with somebody else. I need to be able to lose myself completely in something that isn't work. Then my batteries get recharged and I'm ready to go out with my friends.

Jake, like most A's, enjoys the type of recreation that has some personal benefit attached. A's hate wasting time and find it difficult to do something just because it's fun. A's are *telic* in their approach to play—they like activities to have a clear objective and a clear result. They enjoy strategy games such as chess because these games are challenging as well as relaxing. You pitch your skills against an adversary, and you either win or lose.

The A prefers to work toward a goal, even if the outcome of a leisure activity isn't as immediate as that of a board game. For instance, while O's will go to a health club to unwind and enjoy the adrenaline flow and exertion of a workout, A's are more motivated by the long-term benefits of exercise.

This mind-set makes A's particularly good at sports and athletics. Setting a goal for one's self to do one's best is not as effective as setting a goal that is realistic but slightly beyond one's capacity. Daniel Gould, one of America's leading sports psychologists, points out that

> Goals such as doing one's best, becoming better, and increasing one's strength are least effective. More effective goals include being able to high jump 6 feet 5 inches by the end of the season or increasing one's maximum lift on the bench press to 240 pounds. If athletes are to show performance improvements, specific measurable goals must be set!

A's in sports tend to drive themselves relentlessly. Whether beginners or professionals, they like to set positive goals for themselves. When playing basketball, for instance, A's will zero in on a specific aspect of the game and then work hard on maximum improvement. In their drive for positive goals, their attitude is "I will try to do better," which is always more effective than the negative approach "I will try not to keep making those mistakes."

Harriet, an A homemaker from Boston in her forties, talks about her effective exercise strategies at the gym:

> When I joined the gym last March I had a very clear picture of what I wanted to do. My goal was to lose eight pounds and tone up—to get back some of that teen figure I used to have. I decided the only way to do this would be to give myself little objectives that would be easy enough to reach. So I decided to aim for losing two pounds a week over a month. . . . I'm not the dieting type, and I'm definitely *not* the suffering type. What I did was to eat as much as I always have—even my afternoon muffin with my coffee—but I cut as much fat out of my diet as I possibly could, and started working on the club's treadmill. First five minutes, then ten, and within three weeks I was up to eighteen. I've kept that up ever since. The result was that I surprised myself by achieving my weight-loss goal within three weeks. That was a pleasant surprise! So I tell my friends to set up their goals and then go for it! Sometimes its hard to start something new, like going to the gym four, five times a week—it's quite a step, but it's definitely worth it!

When they approach an unfamiliar area, A's tread carefully. As Harriet puts it, it can be "quite a step." For instance, despite the technology explosion of the 1990s, many A's have stayed away from computers. But once they get the bug, A's become enthusiastic users. As the French psychologist, Léone Bourdel points out, the A "adapts himself with reluctance, living his life according to a plan of constant aspiration for harmony with his environment." The A is pulled by the conflicting needs of belonging and wishing to keep a distance. A's who discover the Internet find that it is an excellent medium through which they can communicate and express themselves. What A's find particularly attractive is that this form of communication is totally unreserved but still controllable. If you get in too deep you press a button and you're out. A's, diffident by nature in a crowd, become remarkably expressive and free in front of their computer screens.

B's at Play

Of all the blood types, the B has the clearest sense of self: If B's want to do something, they do it. Pleasure from work, friends, even family, fades into the background when it's time to play. For the B, leisure activities and hobbies are a private, almost sacrosanct, domain.

Like the A, the B looks above all for challenge and learning in a hobby. They find playing just for the fun of it extremely difficult: Relaxation for them has to be a means to an end. B's want to achieve something in their hobby; they want experiences that can help educate them. More than anything, the B's ideal hobby is a means of self-expression. Like A's, B's are *telic* in their play—they enjoy activities with a clear goal. The B might paint or sculpt or bodybuild—whatever the hobby, the emphasis is more on the result than on getting there. But in their zeal for achieving results, B's are far more driven than A's.

Marty, a B designer from New York, talks about his energetic and creative approach to his hobby, making pottery:

I'm a fashion-jewelry designer, but my hobby is pottery. It's a relatively new hobby; I've only been taking classes for about a year, but since I have a strong background in crafts I'm pleased with the progress I've been making. I head down to the pottery studio three times a week after work and sit at the pottery wheel for about four hours. It's my happiest time. I get totally absorbed. As I work, I see the end product, the beautiful vase or pot that I'm working on, in my mind. And I try to get closer and closer to that image until the piece is ready. When I'm working I lose myself in the process. I get totally centered on the image of what I am trying to create. What's around me is totally blocked out until I'm done—I don't see or hear anything. Then wham! I launch into the next project. I average about two or three pieces per session—which is quite good. Week by week I'm getting faster and better.

When B's immerse themselves in their activities they can reach extraordinary levels of concentration. They can be watching television or arranging stamps or surfing the Internet—once they have committed themselves to doing something, they are totally caught up in it.

This single-minded concentration is a major factor in the B's approach to exercise and sports. The successful sporting B is the type who believes that the mind can effectively control and direct the body. Once B's have decided to do something they really go for it.

The "image," the "result," the "blocked-out" surroundings that Marty describes in his pottery work are all-important elements in reaching one's peak of perfection in athletics. Jack Nicklaus, the world-famous golfing champion, has said that mental preparation is the single most critical element in top performance. Nicklaus, a B, has been quoted as saying that golf is 90 percent mental activity, and sports psychologists believe that his concentration skills have helped him reach a level far above that of other golfers.

Of all the blood types, B's are the least affected by their

environment. Specialists have dubbed them gruff, cool, distant, neurotic. But despite their shortcomings, B's have a narrow focus of attention that causes them to screen out the outside world and concentrate entirely on what they are doing.

B's don't enjoy playing in groups—they like individual sports, where they can follow their own ideas and objectives and shine as individuals. Team sports, such as football, baseball, and ice hockey, need lighting-quick team reactions and decisions. Players have to pay attention to one another, to have a broad spectrum of concentration, because throughout the game they are constantly bombarded by an onslaught of disparate cues from team players and opponents. The pressure is high and reactions have to be quick. B's in team sports fall prey to what the sports world calls "paralysis by analysis": Players mull over what is happening inside themselves instead of paying attention to teammates, opponents, or the ball.

In an individual sport like golf the pressure can be just as high, but the crucial difference for the B is that he or she is the one calling all the shots. Carol, a B painter in her early thirties, says that the "mathematics" of golf, combined with its "die-hard competitiveness," have made her a fanatic player:

> In high school I was a total loser in sports. I ended up on the basketball team because I'm so tall, but as the games went on I'd get slower and duller, and my teammates would be furious. It wasn't a ticket to popularity! So who would have thought I'd become such an avid golfer? It's an amazing sport, and it's *very* competitive in a different way, which is what I really like about it. It's all up to you— you are the one who has to come up with the goods. It's not like basketball, where your game is affected by how good your teammates are. In golf you're out there by yourself, and luck has nothing to do with who wins. All

that matters is which of the players is the cleverest, who's the better mathematician. You try to calculate the wind's strength and its direction, the dampness of the grass, how to avoid the bunkers, and plan all that with your stroke, then you're in business. When I hear people say "Good luck, Carol!" my hair stands on end.

As in Carol's case, the B's persistence and determination often turn their leisure activities into a specialty. Given the right amount of time and space, B's are masters at assessing the demands of a situation and then acting accordingly.

What makes B's best at high-concentration activities is their capacity to identify problem areas and error patterns in their approach and then modify what they do. This comes in handy particularly in technical leisure activities such as computing. B's see their computer terminal as a high-powered link to an endless number of resources. The B with a computer asks, "What can this machine do for me? How can it help me get what I want?"

For B's the computer is a gateway to personal efficiency and success. Software games and surfing for fun on the Internet are low on their itineraries. When linked to cyberspace, the B becomes the ultimate hunter-gatherer, vacuuming up mountains of useful information.

Jeffrey, a B writer in his midtwenties, says that his computer has provided him with a creative boost. Beyond the fun and games of the Internet, a whole world of information is at his fingertips:

> Since I've been computerized, my productivity has soared. Some people still think that serious writers are supposed to compose their magnum opus with a quill pen, preferably in some fashionable café. Bad idea! I have a Dutch writer friend who scoffs at me for using a laptop—but let's

face it, I'm on my fifth book, and he hasn't even finished his first. I'm still amazed at the wealth of information out there in cyberspace. When I need facts for something I'm writing—facts that only a specialist would know, I just fire off a query over the Internet to one of the forums I belong to. For one of my stories I needed to find out about the structure of the box of a pointe shoe, the hard casing that keeps a ballerina on her toes. I was inundated with E-mail! British box constructions, I found out, curve in an arch for an elegant line, but American shoes point straight down. Then there is a pointe-shoe factory south of Minsk which uses a secret mix of paper pulp and glue that is supposed to last longer, and you can buy the shoes wholesale. It would be worth flying there to shop! The information is limitless. With the E-mail I got from these computerized ballerinas I could write a toe-shoe encyclopedia!

O's at Play

The philosopher Aristotle said that "nature requires that we should be able not only to work well but to use leisure well."

Of all the blood types, the O is the one who lives closest to this credo. O's work hard, but they also play hard. Extroverted and outgoing, they have a practical and straightforward approach to leisure activities: If something is fun, why not do it? Recreation, the O feels, is an important change in routine, a necessary break from the stress of work. While other blood types might see work as the "real world" and recreation as peripheral, O's invest as much energy and time as they can in recreation and the "pursuit of happiness."

The O is much more likely than the A or the B to choose a hobby simply because it is enjoyable; there doesn't necessarily have to be a reason for it. In this sense, O's are what social psychologists call *autotelic*: The fun of an activity is more important than the end result or the long-term benefits. O's, for instance, tend to go to the gym because they enjoy the "high" of a workout: Working to achieve a perfect body is usually not enough of a motive.

O's enjoy group leisure and mass leisure most of all. In *Tempéraments psychobiologiques*, the French specialist Gille-Maisani emphasizes the O's enjoyment of and need for social interaction:

> The O is characterized by his good social adaptability. Typically, he is an extrovert with strong social ambition and an open, optimistic, and dynamic approach. He seeks out contacts because they enrich him and he needs them to thrive. By extension, he fears solitude.

For the O, whether with a few good friends at home or among a crowd of strangers at a concert, real recreation is recreation in a group. New contacts can be made, relationships with friends and family strengthened. As Gille-Maisani points out, the O finds it hard to be alone. Solitary recreation for long stretches of time—watching TV, reading, going alone for a drive—is unsettling.

Mark, an O hotel concierge in his midthirties, says that going places, meeting people, and making new friends is his ideal of relaxation:

> I'm not the type who likes to hang out at home after work. I like mixing with people, having fun, having a good time. I've met most of my best friends in galleries, at dance clubs, in cafés. Like tonight, I'm going to hang out with a friend I got to know at Stingy Lulu's restaurant a few months ago. I was sitting there alone when this wild group

of Europeans at the table next to me started talking about a new drag bar called Bardo. Well, that got me going! I turned to them and said, "Excuse me, I couldn't help overhearing . . ." and that started things off. We got talking; they were fascinating. There was a jet-setter model from Switzerland with her friend, a tattooed artist and his brother. One of the drag-queen waitresses even came and sat down with us. We really hit it off well. Sebastian, a graphic designer from Germany, was particularly interesting, and many dinners, dance clubs, and drinks down the line we're still the best of friends.

The O's gravitation to groups makes them natural team players. They are prepared to work with others to reach common goals, which is extremely important for group sports, such as football, basketball, and baseball. As either amateur or professional athletes, O's fit well into the collective identity of a team, where structured patterns of interaction and interdependence are key elements for a good game. As sports psychologists point out, a successful team acts as a group, not a collection of individuals. O's have a natural tendency to what one might call *we-ism* as opposed to *me-ism*. The O perceives the team's objectives as "our goals"—not "my goals," or worse, "their goals."

The O's tendency to choose an activity because it's fun and not because of the advantages it might bring also gives them a healthy edge in athletics. While B's are often *extrinsically motivated* in sports—motivated by the status, the medals, the trophies—O's are generally *intrinsically motivated*: They engage in a sport because they enjoy it. The pleasure they feel while they are involved in a game often makes them more tenacious athletes. While A's and B's often drop out if they don't reach their goals, the O's interest and involvement keeps them going.

All in all, fun is the main prerequisite the O seeks in recreational activities. Whether watching television or playing video games, O's want to be entertained. O's particularly enjoy the limitless entertainment and communication possibilities open to them in cyberspace. At a party you can meet ten or fifteen people, but in cyberspace you can meet thousands. Keiko, an O Japanese-American, says that she is addicted to chat groups on the Internet. She says that in the past few years she has made many "cyberspace friends" with whom she is in regular contact:

> I got my first computer five years ago, and it was love at first sight. I've chewed my way through two machines already, and I'm thinking of getting a new one that's even faster in about three months when the prices drop again. All my life I was a television freak—forget that! With my new interactive CD-ROMs and the chat groups I belong to, if I want home entertainment I know where to turn. I'm addicted to chat groups, so I budget myself on that, but there is so much going on on the Internet! So much stuff is free. I can't see how that's going to last, but as long as it does I intend to use it to the max!

AB's at Play

AB's are often accused of dilettantism. Friends and family are surprised at the speed with which AB's can pick up and drop hobbies. But what often looks like an extreme case of dabbling is actually the AB's enterprising temperament. Leisure is a time for self-expression, for finding oneself, for being creative. As AB's see it, you have to try everything before you can settle down into one activity and stay there.

Once AB's find the perfect leisure activity, they are hooked.

As the Japanese expert Toshitaka Nomi warns, "they are passionate when they are obsessed."

Like B's, AB's who find their ideal hobby become specialists; many turn the hobby into a second career. AB's, more than other blood types, need an outlet for their creativity. If their job doesn't provide it, AB's often make their leisure time the center of their day. For other blood types, leisure may be merely recuperative, "tanking up" so they can go back to work with renewed energy, but for many AB's leisure has a high priority—sometimes even higher than work.

Boris, an AB in his late twenties, says that although he likes his work, his hobby, modern dance, is more important to him than his career in a law firm on Park Avenue. Since he started dancing four years ago he has dropped all his other leisure activities, and dance has become central:

> My passion is modern dance; I'm studying Graham technique. I take two classes a day, sometimes three, although I'm twenty-eight and started kind of late, so I don't see it as ever becoming my profession. I'm an accountant in a law firm. I took a job with this firm because it's flexible: I can work evenings, which gives me a chance to take dance classes in the morning. So, to answer your question, yes, my hobby *is* more important to me than my job. I would never take a job that would get in the way of my dancing. It started kind of by mistake. I was in a car accident and the doctor sent me to a dance therapist to get my back muscles straightened out. I was hooked from the first class! Within six months I left Michigan, because I wanted to take classes at the Graham Studios in New York. I feel like I've found myself in dancing. It's had a great impact on my life.

Boris goes on to say that there are many different facets of his leisure activity that he enjoys. In order to strengthen his technique he also takes dance classes in ballet and jazz. And he works out at a gym for extra upper-body strength: "It's not just the dance, I enjoy all the activities around it, from having coffee with other dancer friends of mine to going to the theater to watch the company perform—that's really great, because I've studied many of the pieces in workshops."

Like all AB's, Boris is attracted to order and system. According to him, dance, like accounting, has strict rules. You either do it right or you don't. As the French psychologist Léone Bourdel points out, AB's feel at sea if they don't keep their many-sided, *complexe*, temperament in check. This goes for work as well as play.

When AB's do something, they are quick to immerse themselves in it completely. As in Boris's case, their "intensity of engagement" is particularly strong. Even in simple, everyday activities such as watching television, the AB is active and intensely involved. AB's are inveterate channel-surfers, but once they alight on a program they really want to watch they focus all their attention on it. It could be a movie, a news program, or a talk show—the AB does not sit back passively and let the information seep in, but interacts with the program. To the AB at play, the length of time is not as important as the quality and intensity of the activity.

In personality tests, the Chinese authority K. H. Mee gave AB's the lowest scores in emotional stability, but the highest in intuition and carefulness. The AB's eye for detail and quick reaction to changes in their environment make them especially good at high-speed interactive sports like hockey, basketball, football, and soccer. AB's are highly sensitive to the slightest external cue and are good at focusing their attention and quickly processing the large amounts of information that pour in from all sides during these games: their opponents' positions, their teammates' moves, the ball's potential direction.

The quick and sensitive reactions of AB's make them good

with machinery. Like B's, AB's see machines from household appliances to high-powered computers as excellent tools for widening the scope of what they can do. The *complexe* AB has a *complexe* approach to software. Once addicted to their computers, AB's find them hard to resist: AB's often become self-proclaimed *commodity fetishists*—if a program is on the market they have to have it. AB's often find themselves looking for the perfect program that is guaranteed to enhance their scope on the computer. Owning as many programs as possible becomes a symbol of all the potential of which the computer is capable.

John, an AB professor of comparative literature, says that for him the computer occupies a central position in both work and play. He says that keeping pace with technology is important to him—he can't resist an upgrade or a new machine:

> We academics have been somewhat slow on getting computerized—even many of our graduate students are lagging behind. For me the computer has made a world of difference. Things that used to take weeks, I can now do in an hour! I do everything on my computer, from organizing lectures and writing articles and books to E-mailing friends and colleagues worldwide. I don't belong to any forums, but I like surfing through all the home pages having to do with literature. My view is, if you own a machine, you should get to know it. So in a nutshell, hiking and my computer are my two hobbies in life. And when it comes to my hobbies I don't hold back. I regularly fly to Europe for a long hiking weekend, and when there is a new software product or upgrade on the market, I'm the first in line to buy it. Since the mideighties I've been getting a newer, better model every three years, on average. I usually donate my old computers to students.

EPILOGUE

Today research is taking blood typing even further as hematologists continue to isolate hundreds of blood factors within each group. The relation between blood markers and psychology is being explored in ever greater depth. The whole field of knowledge is about to open up in the West. Every aspect of human thought and action is being studied—even left-handedness, smoking, and drinking habits. I am carrying on with my own work, on the one hand keeping in touch with the latest science, and on the other continuing to develop ways to help people understand themselves better.